Full Bloom

Full Bloom

Thoughts from an Opinionated Gardener

Rayford Clayton Reddell

Illustrations by Lourdes Livingston

HARMONY BOOKS/NEW YORK

Published by Harmony Books, a division of Crown Publishers, Inc., 201 East 50th Street, New York, New York 10022.
Member of the Crown Publishing Group.
Random House, Inc.
New York, Toronto, London, Sydney, Auckland
http://www.randomhouse.com/

HARMONY and colophon are trademarks of Crown Publishers, Inc.

Manufactured in the United States of America
Design by Barbara Balch

Library of Congress Cataloging-in-Publication Data is available upon request.

ISBN 0-517-70337-8

10   9   8   7   6   5   4   3   2   1

First Edition

For Bobby

Contents

2 Gardening Tips

3 Dining on the Garden

4 Her Majesty, the Rose

5 Gardening for Fragrance

6 Garden Jewels

7 'Tis the Season

Preface

When Liz Lufkin of the *San Francisco Chronicle* called me in August 1991 to discuss the possibility of my becoming a garden columnist for the paper, she asked about my interest in gardening beyond that of my beloved roses.

"Well, roses *are* my long suit," I admitted, "but thanks to Bob Galyean (the finest gardener I've ever known), I've learned plenty about fragrant plants and a fair amount about garden plants at large. Still," I cautioned, "I'm nothing if not opinionated, and I don't mince words about my attitude toward anything I grow."

"Oh, we don't shy from opinions," she quickly responded.

We decided to give the prospect a try, and I've written a column called "Full Bloom" for the newspaper every other Wednesday since.

I've learned that the gardening world welcomes firm floral attitudes more often than not, though when I step on toes, they sometimes scream. Once, for instance, when I made disparaging remarks about a rose named 'Jiminy Cricket', a reader wrote to inform me, in no uncertain terms, that it was her grandmother's favorite rose and hers, too, and that

I should keep such opinions to myself. Although I've never said another cross word about 'Jiminy Cricket', my attitude toward the dud hasn't altered. To each his own.

Besides my late partner Bob Galyean, I also owe thanks to Victor Yool (a.k.a. "Dr. Hort") for being my personal garden guru; he's taught me plenty.

I'm indebted to the staff of the *San Francisco Chronicle*, especially Rosalie Wright—not only for her staunch support, but for never flinching on the paper's stand on opinions.

Finally, I owe thanks to the dream team at Harmony Books for publishing this collection of columns with the belief that my biases have merit beyond the San Francisco Bay Area.

Rayford Clayton Reddell
Petaluma, California

PART **1**

The Opinionated Gardener

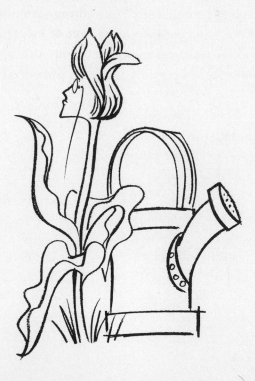

Firm Floral Attitudes

When a recent visitor to my rose beds chastised me for saying ugly things about a particular rose I despise, I pointed out that there are more than 16,000 separately named varieties of roses in commerce.

"How could I possibly think the same of all of them?" I asked.

"Well, of course, you don't have to *think* the same of all of them, but why not just say that the ones you don't like are okay?" my visitor proposed.

The reason I stubbornly persist with my strong views is that okay roses just aren't good enough, considering that they're as much trouble to grow as sensational roses. Who wants to precisely plant, lustily fertilize, water just to the point of excess, and painstakingly prune a bush that produces okay flowers? No, thank you; I'll continue to state that 'Tropicana' will never grow in my garden and that it should be illegal to propagate 'Sterling Silver'. I'm even considering initiating a campaign against 'Chrysler Imperial' (the rose, not the car).

My reasons for so intensely disliking these roses is based on experience with growing them as an adult, but strong horticultural opinions came easy to me. I started forming them as a child. I took a strong dislike to gladioli, for instance, before I reached puberty. In Louisiana, where I grew up, gladioli are as integral to funerals as cemeteries. Even when gladioli blossomed in otherwise cheerful gardens, they reminded me of the dead, and I hated their coarse colors and the tedious composition of their florets.

Louisiana got me off on the wrong foot with other flowers, too, such as canna lilies, gardenias, chrysanthemums, wisterias, and zinnias.

I hated where canna lilies grew more than I disliked the flowers themselves. Since Louisiana has ridiculously abundant rainfalls, deep drainage ditches crisscross the state. Anything growing in these swampy troughs had better tolerate plenty of water during rainfalls, and wallowing hogs in between. Until I was in grade school, I thought that ditches were created for pigs and those plants called cannas with the mangled leaves and tacky crepe paper flowers.

Gardenias grow wild in Louisiana, particularly in cemeteries where potted plants are placed at grave sites. Because the subtropical muggy climate is so ideal for them, hungry gardenia plants thrust out tendrils from the bottoms of their containers to root in any nearby soil. Ironically, the problem with an abundance of gardenias is the very reason people covet them—fragrance. Gardenias are powerfully scented, and the perfume of too many at once is over-powering and can even induce nausea.

I graduated from high school before learning that there was more to the world of chrysanthemums than floppy, oversized autumnal blooms pinned to the chests of female football fans. As for wisteria, I reached manhood before knowing that vines could climb on supports other than trees, which they ultimately choke.

I moved to California before I began to like zinnias. In south Louisiana, zinnias are planted in riotous clashes of color that make you want to look the other way. Even as a young boy, I wondered why no one ever thought of keeping zinnia seeds separated by color.

Now my opinions, although still strong, are tempered. For instance, I cultivate species canna lilies and marvel at their intensely green but still translucent leaves and the majesty of their lusciously colored long-stemmed blossoms. Instead of groves of perfume-doused gardenias, I prefer single plants and solitary blooms. Chrysanthemums, I've learned, are a widely divergent family, including many varieties that are tastefully sized rather than garishly huge. Similarly, wisterias now look out of place when growing in trees instead of on arches, drain pipes, or over whole sheds, and all my zinnias grow in patches of one color.

I still hate gladioli.

Speaking Proper
Horticultural Lingo

A lthough it took longer than it should have for me to admit it, I'm now convinced that if you have the slightest intention of becoming serious about gardening, you have no choice but to learn some horticultural lingo.

I used to skirt the issue because of my single-mindedness about the labeling of roses—not in proper Latin, but rather, by some name their hybridizer dreamed up, like 'Color Magic', 'Pristine', 'Peaudouce', 'Fragrant Cloud', or 'Dolly Parton'. Then I became interested in fragrant plants and quickly learned that common names would no longer do the trick if I were serious about planting precisely what I had in mind—fragrant sweet peas, for instance.

"Oh, Rayford, pick me up a package of sweet pea seeds when you're at the store," my mother would say when I was a boy in Louisiana. Although I didn't save one to prove it, I'm sure those packets were labeled "sweet peas," period. (I'm also certain that they were all fragrant.)

Later, I moved to California and started hobnobbing with sophisticated botanical types who assured me that, although there are more than one hundred species of sweet peas, only one is fragrant—*Lathyrus odoratus*. Pardon me.

I suffered similar put-downs over daphne, lavender, thyme, birch trees, even magnolia—Louisiana's state flower. Once, when all I wanted was a white wisteria, I was informed by a haughty nurseryman that I must choose then and there between *Wisteria venusta* and *W. sinensis* 'Alba'. Under pressure, I chose the wrong one.

So many plants are known as mock orange that you must never ask for it by that name alone. Only *Philadelphus* legitimately deserves this sobriquet, yet everything that smells remotely like citrus ends up being called mock orange.

Botanical names of plants and their families, such as *Asclepiadaceae, Dispsacaceae,* and *Hamamelidaceae,* can be next to impossible to pronounce. Even when you finally get them right, they don't sound right, and a name you would swear you had committed to memory one day won't come to you the next day for the world.

A major problem with botanical names is that they keep changing, especially among plants whose offspring have become too numerous to track. The *Datura* clan, for instance, has now officially been split in half, with only the annual version retaining the family name; the perennials now go by *Brugmansia*.

Another reason for giving in to botonical names is that a plant called by a certain common name in one place is called another name elsewhere. For instance, what is periwinkle in England and myrtle on the East Coast goes around as vinca (also the proper name) in California.

Fortunately, the common and botanical names of some plants are the same, like buddleia (the butterfly bush) and freesia. Other names, such as hyacinths (properly *Hyacinthus*), differ by a single letter. The botanical and proper names of many plants, however, have nothing whatsoever to do with each other. Wallflowers are properly called *Cheiranthus*, lilacs are *Syringa*, and pinks and carnations are *Dianthus*. Some common names hint at what the proper names might be. Bay, for instance, is often called laurel, helping you to remember the correct genus name of *Laurus*. But then you must also remember to tack on the species name, *nobilis*, when you go shopping, for *Laurus nobilis* is the bay with which you want to scent your garden and flavor your cooking.

Learning how to properly pronounce fancy botanical names has become easier thanks to publications like *American Horticulturist*, which includes a foolproof pronunciation guide at the end of each issue. Recalling those names on cue is another matter.

When I'm in the company of horticulturists well versed in matters nomenclatural, I do a lot of bluffing when my memory (or knowledge) fails me. "Which variety is this," I might ask when I can't even remember the genus. If I suspect the plant in question is something radically offbeat, I follow Christopher Lloyd's advice and without blinking inquire, "What are you calling this nowadays?"

The Green Thumb Myth

Since it has always irked me deeply that no one ever said I have a green thumb, I'm delighted to inform you that there is no such thing. Gardeners aren't born with an innate ability to command plants to flourish or to distinguish petunia seedlings from baby crabgrass; we learn our way around gardens the way good cooks come to sashay about a kitchen.

When I grew up in Louisiana, my mother was the gardening heroine of the family. "With that green thumb of hers, Saih can make anything grow," my aunts oohed in admiration. Once, when I spotted an emerald fleck on her thumb, I imagined I finally found evidence that my mother's thumbs actually were green, but it turned out to be a piece of scallion that missed her pot of gumbo.

When I turned my hands to gardening, I learned that this God-given blessing attributed to my mother and other gardeners who seemingly worked outdoor miracles was nothing more than keen eyes casing what conditions certain plants preferred: how much sun, when they wanted it most, and how much water how often.

The principles of good gardening can be gleaned from books, of course, but nothing beats firsthand experience, particularly in your own garden. At the risk of sounding like an old geezer, when novice gardeners tell me that they've just bought a home with space for a garden that they can hardly wait to tend, I beg them to hold off on major plantings for a year. "Get to know your land," I urge, "including when the sun shines where and for how long." What appears in February to be a perfect spot for roses or other sun lovers may be cast in shade by June when that deciduous tree leafs out. A dry corner of the garden, which seemed like a haven for bearded iris last May, may be waterlogged next March and cause iris rhizomes to rot. If neighbors keep a night-light burning just adjacent to the spot you've selected for chrysanthemums, look somewhere else since chrysanthemums bloom after long dark nights, and extended periods of light confuse them.

To "green" your thumb, get accustomed to the fact that certain garden terminology only sounds threatening but actually isn't, like *pH*—the number on a scale of 14 that reveals acidic/alkaline properties, or how sweet the soil is. The lower the pH, the more acidic the soil; the higher the pH, the more alkaline the soil. This pH value isn't something sophisticated gardeners toss around simply to strut their stuff; it's basic to selecting happy garden spots for certain plants. If you read, for instance, that rhododendron and azalea like acid soils (which they do), realize that you'll doubtlessly have to punch up your ground with leaf mold and peat moss, additives that heighten acidity. On the contrary, if you yearn to grow lilac, but hear that lilac prefers alkaline soil, reach for a bag of lime—a surefire acid counteragent.

Plants differ maddeningly in how much water they like to drink; your recognizing of these needs leads to good companion plantings. Roses were born thirsty and yearn for stiff drinks from April through October. Contrarily, most herbs (like lavender, rosemary, and thyme) appreciate a modicum of water and reach their peak of bloom or flavor only when stressed with thirst. If you plant any of these herbs at the feet of your roses, you declare war on your garden and demand that your hose keep it all straight.

As your acumen grows, you will think it second nature to keep aphid infestations at a minimum by scattering plantings of garlic. Lay out vegetable patches by choosing beneficial neighbors that enhance each other's taste, like cucumbers do lettuce and radishes do beans; have nearby a supply of common sand for improving the soil where tender cuttings are expected to root; even turn mature hydrangeas from pink to blue by tossing aluminum sulfate at their feet.

When you master such garden trickery, someone is likely to say that you surely were born with a green thumb. You know you weren't, of course, but accept such praise anyway; I certainly would.

Suffering the Humiliation of Exhibition

Although I've gardened for years, the only flowers I have ever exhibited are roses. Once I had a drawer full of blue, red, and yellow ribbons to prove my blooms deserved first, second, or third prizes. I quit exhibiting. Now I wonder whatever possessed me to endure the humiliation inflicted by judges who not only declare when blossoms deserve recognition, but also why they don't.

I began with a bang. The schedule for my first rose show included a category for three separate stems of one variety of Grandiflora rose in a single container. I cut three fine stems of the Chinese lacquer red 'Ole' rose, plunked them in a bud vase, and set them on the show table. To my great delight, the judges draped a blue ribbon around the neck of the container. I was hooked.

I learned that my 'Ole' roses had earned five points toward the twenty required to elevate me to the amateur class, and I ached for fifteen more, which I easily won on my second try—not all first places, but a sufficient number of seconds and thirds to graduate from novice status.

The going got rougher when I competed with amateur peers. Even so, my finest competitive moment ever came when my rose won Queen of the Show (the highest award given to a single blossom entered in a rose show) with the majestic 'John F. Kennedy' Hybrid Tea rose. "Magnificent," the judges called my stunning entry, as they awarded it enough points to exalt me to the advanced amateur class. I was set up for the kill.

Once you become an advanced amateur, judges consider you tough enough to endure catty comments scribbled on the back of entry tags. "A bud is not a bloom," the judges said of my Floribunda 'Angel Face' that hadn't unfurled sufficient rows of petals to suit them. Of a dinner-plate-sized blossom of the sinfully perfumed 'Fragrant Cloud', some judge wrote, "this rose is overfertilized—notice the exaggerated foliage." Exaggerated, my foot! I quit exhibiting and fertilized to my heart's content.

Recently, I learned that roses aren't the only flowers ill-humored judges pick apart. Last spring, I attended a flower show held at a fancy gift store, where pots of bulbs were entered for competition. The tag for each entry was large enough to accommodate the entrant's name and address and the judges' comments. "This exhibit would benefit from more foliage," an ornery judge said of a pot of lovely paperwhites. Although it had, admittedly, less foliage than the winning entry, it was still a knockout and undeserving of faint contempt. I couldn't help wondering if Mrs. Whozis would ever exhibit again and subject her lovely paper-whites to such nasty comments for all her friends to read.

Bitchier words were there, too. A container of superb tulips were said to be "off-centered and overpotted"; lovely amaryllis were deemed to be of "insipid color"; and a stand of handsome cyclamen that I'd give my eyeteeth to have grown were called no more than "a good start." A pot of daffodils showing telltale signs of snail and aphid damage was thought to have "enough livestock to start a small farm."

Still, I'll bet the losers from this show continue to exhibit, at least until they've won enough ribbons to assure themselves that they grow their pet flowers to perfection. I might reenter the showring myself. After all, my bushes of 'John F. Kennedy' have been showing off lately, and I can't resist wondering what those snotty judges would have to say about their blossoms. They are oversized, though.

Oh, to hell with competition—I'll just polish the trophy I already have.

Coexisting with Pets in the Garden

∞

I suspect that a recent visitor to my garden saw *Sophie's Choice* once too often because she asked one of the dumbest questions I've ever heard: "If you had to give up one or the other, would you keep your pets or your garden?"

Instead of properly chastising her for posing such an agonizing thought, I told her that I couldn't tolerate that decision, and switched the subject to the plant she was standing on.

My garden and I live with three pets. Although our cohabitation isn't entirely blissful, neither is it disrespectful. Sadie, a German shorthair dog, has been here the longest and she's the best behaved. The garden, however, suffered from Sadie's puppyhood. She loved to dig wherever anything was just planted and relished rolling over freshly seeded lawns because they smelled of aged manure. As she matured, Sadie came to respect the intent of paths and stayed on them. Even when she didn't understand why she should stand on a rough path of gravel instead of rolling in soft beds of annuals, she finally did it anyway.

Still, after twelve years of telling her not to, Sadie loves to lie in the center of perennials in full bloom—acidanthera, for instance. Sadie doesn't give a hoot about acidanthera while it's growing; she prances by clumps with no notice of young swordlike leaves. Then, once sheathlike stems burst into fragrant blossom, Sadie finds acidanthera irresistible and wiggles right to the center of the most lush specimen she can find. Once they've got a load of Sadie, few stems ever stand erect again.

Sheena, our Manx cat, came to the garden after we could no longer stay ahead of the gophers. For the first six years of her life, Sheena was a terrific gopher hunter. Then, she settled into an easy life of dry Science Diet. Still, to her credit, our gopher infestation has been decimated.

The only time Sheena was ever a problem in the garden was when I carelessly spread mature plants of catnip among other herbs. Big mistake. If catnip is planted from seed, cats have no way of finding it. Only when mature plants are bruised or when they begin to dry do they leak the oil that drives cats into a frenzy. Once cats sniff it, they can't get enough. They plunge their noses into it, roll on it, scratch at it, and rip out entire plantings in an orgasmic effort to rub the oil into their fur. I grew catnip long before Sheena went nuts that day, but always kept it on the insides of large beds of thyme and chives, neither of which interests her. Even when the catnip became established, the cat didn't find it because it remained unbruised.

Margo, an African gray parrot, is the most troublesome of my trio of pets. She'll eat anything, but her favorite is wisteria. Except at night, or days when temperatures dip below freezing, or skies pelt rain, Margo lives outdoors on a large 100-year-old grapevine that's hung from pillars framing a sundeck. Those same pillars serve as hosts for vines of wisteria. Even when the bowls on her vine are ripe with food, Margo prefers wisteria. I pluck off seed pods, of course, because they're poisonous, but otherwise, Margo insists on clipping the wisteria herself.

I've come to terms with my three ladies. I keep acidanthera staked, not because they need help staying upright, but because Sadie doesn't like to lie down around stakes. I still grow catnip, but in two patches—Sheena's is beyond harm's way and mine is well secreted behind a hedge of rosemary (Sheena doesn't like the smell of turpentine, which rosemary freely releases).

As for Miss Margo, it's far easier to train the wisteria.

Fabulous Floral Flair

I've always deeply admired people who have natural design sense in the garden because I don't. Although I sometimes choose companion plantings that people tell me work out well, they usually weren't my idea first, but rather my version of what I saw and liked in someone else's garden. I've never visited Sissinghurst, for instance, without returning home with intentions of duplicating a tiny piece of that fabulous place. Sissinghurst is the horticultural triumph of Vita Sackville-West, a British gardening daredevil who not only used color to perfection, but also had an unerring flair for combining plants simply for their contrasting (or similar) growth habits, or for texture in their leaves, like pairing *Choisya ternata* (Mexican orange) with *Galium odoratum* (sweet woodruff) because their similarly formed whorls of foliage and tiny white flowers flatter each other.

Until ten years ago, I observed such talent only from afar. Then, I began gardening with Robert Galyean, a fine gardening photographer, and saw flair in action, firsthand. Bob and I shared a garden of heirloom roses. Selecting the dowager roses was my responsibility; finding them suitable companions was his.

When Bob told me that he had decided on ornamental grasses as the plant to be featured among the rosebushes, I told him he was crazy. I remembered German gardens with a few grasses near roses, but grasses as a feature? Somehow I doubted that roses and grasses belonged together any more than wisteria and pineapples do. Besides, how could I allow Gold Band pampas grass to grow behind my sophisticated butter-yellow English rose 'Graham Stuart Thomas' or New Zealand flax at its feet?

Finally I admitted that the fact I had never seen roses and grasses flourishing side by side didn't mean I wouldn't like the combination, and Bob planted what he knew was right all along.

When antique roses blossom, which most of them do only once each year, no one ever wonders what's planted beneath or beside their shrubs—all eyes fix on the roses. Then, after about six weeks of glory, excitement subsides and people begin noticing that those rosebushes have leggy bottoms and foliage unworthy of scrutiny all summer. That's when ornamental grasses take over.

Because most ornamental grasses should be sheared to the ground in late winter (just before spring forces them to rise again), they're still short when once-blooming roses blossom. When the roses subside, as if on cue, grasses begin to stretch outward and upward, sending their shoots into openings among neighboring plants, often with complementary effects.

Shrubs weren't the only roses that Bob introduced like a born matchmaker. We built a colonnade through the center of the garden with spaces for forty-two climbing roses. I agonized for months on just which roses they should be and finally decided to mix only six varieties—two deep pinks, two soft pinks, and two near whites. Safe choices.

It was soon obvious that the limits I had placed on the number of rose varieties didn't faze Bob's intentions for selecting clematises to accompany them. Whereas I was honed my rose list to six, Bob couldn't get his clematis selection below twenty varieties.

The sheer number didn't bother me, but the range of colors did. I wondered how it could be correct to have 'Zephirine Drouhin' (a hot pink, deliciously perfumed Bourbon rose) paired with the translucent white clematis 'John Huxtable' on one column and with the violet blue 'Gipsy Queen' on another. The thought of clematis with star-shaped flowers next to informal blossoms of the buff-white Noisette rose 'Madame Alfred Carrière' was appealing, but wine red? I remembered the grasses and kept faith. You should see that colonnade in bloom!

I've always wondered whether, if I had chosen twenty varieties of climbing roses, Bob would have suggested only six clematises to tie them together. He said he wasn't sure, that he'd have had to look at the roses before deciding.

That's how gardeners with flair are.

Color Your Garden
Carefully

∞

When most people begin gardening, they have but one goal in mind—to make plants grow. Although horticultural newcomers may be keenly sensitive to color combinations indoors, their gardens are often another matter. "I wish I hadn't planted my purple lilac bushes so close to that hedge of orange wallflowers," they regret, "maybe they won't bloom together next year." They will, of course.

Interior decorators tell gardening friends that they should have borrowed color wheels. "What made you think you'd like purple next to orange in the garden any more than you do in the den?" decorators ask, smirking. Sheepish gardeners confess that they never truly expected the lilacs to live, much less flourish.

When gardeners in search of color harmony comb horticultural references, the name of Gertrude Jekyll keeps popping up. This Miss Jekyll possessed an unerring sense of color. History also documents that her visual acuity worsened severely as she aged, to the point that in her later years she couldn't discern form—only color (which may actually have enhanced her flair). Jekyll's forte was the herbaceous border. According to her, edges of garden borders should be composed of plants with gray foliage. Then, starting at one end of the border, blues should be planted, followed by pale yellows and pinks (both in masses and intergroupings). Color should next pass through stronger yellows, orange, and finally red, at which point the middle of the border should be reached. Then, color strength should recede in an inverse sequence to the opposite end.

Consistent with the budgets of her landed-gentry clients, Gertrude Jekyll gardened on a grand scale. Still, much of what she dictated regarding color can be tastefully applied to gardens of any size, particularly that colors next to each other on a color wheel belong next to each other in the garden, too.

Jekyll also taught us that opposing colors can actually work together, if used in the right amounts. A single scarlet poppy, for instance, can bring to life an entire sea of pale blue campanulas, whereas an equal number of poppies would make the campanulas look dull.

You'll bless the day you decide to keep color groups together—reds with pinks, yellows with orange, blues with mauve, and whites and grays for transition. When chosing color schemes, consider also when you plan to enjoy your garden most and how much light it gets. If you have lots of sun and are home to enjoy it, vivid colors work. Purple and blue flowers, on the other hand, look best in dappled shade. If you enjoy your garden only in the evening, by all means consider white flowers because no color is more beautiful at twilight or in moonlight.

If you want your garden to feel cool, plant lavenders and blues. If you're after warmth, consider yellows and reds. Remember, however, that red is not simply hot, it's riveting—the first color eyes fix on in a spectrum. Especially when combined with yellow (an abrupt contrast), red should be used sparingly, especially in small gardens where drama is out of place. Similarly, most blues are at odds with yellow, and orange fights with mauve.

An interior designer once taught me a trick for assuring that strongly contrasting colors work in the garden. "Make certain that some, however small, portion of a vividly colored flower relates to a color element of its neighbor," she said. "For instance, if you want brilliant blue underneath that stark white 'Iceberg' rose of yours, then plant a lobelia as blue as you like, as long as it has a white center. You can't imagine what a difference those white eyes will make." She was correct, of course, and even though I understood why it happened, I stood amazed that clumps of azure blue lobelia so nicely complemented icy-white roses.

The longer I tend plants, the more I appreciate what foliage does for the garden. In the words of Louise Beebe Wilder, America's answer to Gertrude Jekyll, "In crowding our color groups one against the other, we do not give ourselves opportunity to appreciate the full beauty of any."

Leave room for green, nature's weaver of color.

Pretty in Pink

When I began gardening, I had an aversion to pink flowers.

"You've simply got to get over this weird macho trip you're on," a gardening friend advised, "especially with your interest in roses. More great roses are pink than any other color." My friend proved eminently correct. Beginning with species roses and progressing through every major family that led to modern hybrids, pink is rose's long suit.

Once I got over growing it in the rose garden, pink seemed at home elsewhere, too, especially after I discovered that, like roses, many flowers reach their greatest stage of beauty when they flower in a shade of pink.

Members of the dianthus family, for instance, blossom in a wide array of colors from white to deep red and purple, but those harboring the strongest perfume are often pink—hence, the nickname of dianthus: pink.

Although rhododendrons are being hybridized at an alarming rate, gardeners are loath to part with their floriferous plants of Pink Pearl, an old-timer that flowers in trusses of fat blossoms that look like cotton candy. Ironically, Pink Pearl is also the name of a treasured variety of apple tree, which bears fruit with a delicious soft-pink flesh.

Pink is also at home with a host of annuals, biennials and perennials: verbena, alstromeria, snapdragon, wallflower, stock, phlox, daphne, campanula, foxglove, hellebore, hydrangea, petunia, peony, sweet pea, pansy, and begonias, to name only a handful of garden staples. When varieties of these favorites are also fragrant, a good portion of them will range in color from cool to hot pink. Often, fragrance aside, the cultivars that grow tallest or are adamantly disease resistant happen to be pink. *Oenothera Berlandieri* (commonly called Mexican evening primrose), for instance, is available with either white or pink flowers, but plants of the latter not only grow larger, but also bloom more profusely.

Pink is well represented in exotic flowers, too, and not always where expected. When most gardeners think of fruit-bearing passion vines, for instance, *Passiflora edulis* come to mind, with its purple and white flowers, followed by delicious, deep-purple 3-inch fruit. Another variety, however, *P. mollissima,* not only produces fruit, but has lovely, 3-inch tubular, rose-shaded flowers (it also sets fruit in chilly climates where the *edulis* species won't). Yet another variety, *P. Jamesonii,* bears no fruit, but blossoms all summer in pink shades ranging from salmon to coral.

When I confessed to one of my garden gurus that I had settled on wisteria for planting on a pergola around two sides of my house, but already had enough mauve and white varieties, he suggested pink. Even though I had never seen them in bloom, I knew pink was the ticket.

Although my pink beauties represent a tiny fraction of the total number of wisteria vines I cultivate, more visitors comment on them than those of any other color. It's wonderful to watch reactions. At first, many people say "look what a pretty color this wisteria has faded to." Then, on closer inspection, they realize the decidedly pink flowers haven't faded at all; rather, they're turgid with freshness.

My pergola has also taught me why movie stars like being photographed under pink lights. When those wisterias bloom in front of the many windows looking out to them, the entire house is cast in a pink glow that is flattering to anyone inside—a definite plus.

I've traveled full circle where pink is concerned, horticulturally speaking. Now, my very favorite rose, 'Color Magic', isn't merely pink, its petals are a dazzling blend of shades ranging from baby pink to dusty rose. My spring order for bulbs always includes pink varieties, when available. And, of course, neither love nor money could take those wisterias away.

Dynamic Duos

Soon after I became seriously interested in horticulture, I realized that a visit to England's great gardens was a must. Foremost was Sissinghurst, the jewel of a garden created by Vita Sackville-West and Harold Nicholson in County Kent, England. I had read so much about Sissinghurst that I thought I already knew it by heart.

My arrival was just as expected from the many photographs I had seen of the handsome entrance just under the castle tower. The climbing roses interspersed with the clematis covering the warm brick walls were also precisely as promised. Then I walked away from the castle entrance, toward the moat that borders one end of the garden. Finally, I turned right and skidded to a halt. Before me was the most dynamic garden duo I had ever seen. Never one to shy from gutsy color combinations, Vita had planted deciduous azaleas in shades ranging from pale lemon yellow to vivid apricot orange. At their feet were sky- to lapis-blue forget-me-nots. I groped for my camera.

My second favorite blooming rivalry lives on a country lane near where I garden. There, a three-room cottage looks as though it might collapse were it not for the mature Japanese mauve-to-purple wisteria and bright yellow Banksia roses binding it together. For eleven months of the year, passersby pay no attention to these plants; they're strictly foliar, or deciduous. But, on or about the first of April, they transform the lean-to into the Taj Mahal.

Both species are house eaters and resolved to outperform any flower planted nearby. When paired, they stage a three-week compromise: week one belongs to the wisteria, week three to the rose, but the middle week is a standoff.

If you're willing to flow with the color of the season, good pairings make themselves obvious. Where I garden, for instance, yellow is the signature color of early spring and represented no better than by acacia and daffodils. Their shades of yellow look terrific together, especially when further complemented by blinding-green spring grass.

Clever gardeners use plants with a fickle nature toward pairing, such as *Erysimum* 'Bowle's Mauve', a workhorse of a bloomer that mates happily three times a year. I sentence 'Bowle's Mauve' to annual hard labor in a bed planted with flowering cherry trees, King Alfred daffodils, and fleabane.

Some people find the combination of chrome-yellow daffodils and bright mauve spikes of Erysimum flowers shocking. (I think it's spiffy.) No one, however, quarrels with the color combination created when the fresh pink cherry trees bloom. (Personally, I believe it's almost too tasteful.) The fleabane is a crowd pleaser, probably because the daisylike flowers of *Erigeron* 'Moerheim' are blushed with the same shade of mauve as the Erysimum.

Good pairings—such as rosemary with silver thyme, lavender with hyssop, and santolina with curry plant—make the herb garden a snap for finding comely companions. If you grow nasturtiums for their edible blossoms, consider planting borage nearby. Borage flowers are edible, too, but even more important, their fuzzy, star-shaped sky-blue flowers flatter nasturtium blossoms.

Before planting combinations you dream up yourself, make certain their flowers bloom at the same time. Most of the duos mentioned here will blossom simultaneously no matter where they're planted; they'll simply bloom sooner in USDA Zone 9 than in Zone 8, and months before Zone 5 comes alive.

If you doubt the wisdom of a floral combination you dream up, notice if the two flowers share a single element of color. Blazing-yellow alpine wallflowers, for instance, look riveting when planted near flowers that blossom bloodred because the center of each daisy is mahogany.

Try your hand at garden matchmaking. You may pair quarrelers, but you might introduce bosom buddies.

Horticultural Alchemy

∽

Although most gardeners subscribe to the axiom that it's not nice to mess with Mother Nature, plant breeders scoff at the warning. Determined to discover new colors, sizes, and blooming habits, hybridizers have devised schemes for altering the genes of those flowers they so yearn to improve. In case you don't fully grasp the trickery of such horticultural alchemy, it's important to understand certain basic terminology.

Plants that are candidates for genetic makeover differ in the number of sets of chromosomes in the nucleus of their plant cells. Diploids have two sets of chromosomes; tetraploids, four. Should hybridizers unwittingly mate a diploid with a tetraploid, they may well produce a comely offspring, but it will surely be sterile and useless for further breeding—the reason why the coveted *Rosa rugosa,* kidnapped from China in the late eighteenth century, proved to be a dud for grandfathering a new race of roses until the 1970s, when the diploid-tetraploid mystery was finally unraveled.

Similar roadblocks have hampered development of new strains in other flowers, too. Modern daffodils, for instance, came into being only after the notorious golden-yellow King Alfred variety was hybridized. Because the ubiquitous King Alfred proved to be a tetraploid, the extra set of chromosomes gave hybridizers precisely what they were longing for.

Breeders of irises encountered the same tetraploidy barricade. Although the first tetraploid iris was white—not the color hybridizers sought—it opened the door for future developments that finally led to the coveted pure-pink modern iris. From that date forward, riots of color have emerged among irises.

Hybridizing shenanigans for roses, daffodils, and irises, however, are but a day in the shade compared to what daylily breeders have been up to—they've resorted to poison! The poison that daylily breeders favor for tricking diploids into tetraploidy is colchicine, a toxic and carcinogenic alkaloid derived from *Colchicum autumnale* (meadow saffron). Although it's possible to treat the entire fan of a mature daylily with colchicine, the preferred treatment involves working simultaneously with thousands of seeds on the brink of germination.

Daylily breeders swear that the only way they know if they are using enough colchicine is to keep adding it to their washes until at least 70 percent of the seeds die. Even then, the vast majority of survivors (more than 25 percent) will stubbornly remain diploids. With luck, perhaps as many as 3 percent will actually convert to tetraploids. As if those percentages weren't discouraging enough, several converts will prove to be sterile, in which case they might just as well have remained diploids since they'll never parent exciting children of their own.

Why would anyone go to all this bother? The answer lies in the enormous increase in positive characteristics of potential offspring—not just color and size, but also thicker and more luminous petals and foliage with greater substance.

Considering what a pain they are to discover, it's no surprise that daylily introductions fetch prices up to $250 each. In time, assuming new cultivars prove to be popular enough to propagate in large numbers, their cost will dwindle to as low as, say, $5 per division.

Before you decide that people who wash their daylily seeds in colchicine must be insane, take a look at some of their results. Hybridizers of daylilies have not only come up with butter-yellow varieties like Spiderweb and Carol I. Colossal, whose blossoms reach widths greater than 10 inches each, they've graced our gardens with miniature varieties, skyscrapers of more than 4 feet, and several cultivars that bloom over a ten-month period. I wouldn't be surprised if the next catalog I open offers a blue daylily. Why not? I think *I'd* turn blue if someone threatened me with a wash of alkaline poison.

Think Big, Plant Small

A decade ago, when I planted my present garden, I enlisted the help of a landscape designer. All plants considered, his vision for a garden at maturity was 20/20 and I greatly value most (but not all) of his advice. For instance, I spent a small fortune for several established plants that I'm still paying for, horticulturally speaking.

"Don't make people wonder what that hedge of bay will look like in a few years," he firmly suggested. "Give guests a glimpse right away by planting a few specimens here and there"—advice that translated into the purchase of expensive established trees plus the seedlings in five-gallon containers I could afford.

Once the bays were planted, I understood his foresight. "These will soon look like those," I assured visitors, as I pointed to the tiny plants hovering at ground level, then at those towering over my head.

Now, the problem is that "these" look better than "those." The *Laurus nobilis* (bay's true name) that I bought as adult trees not only have gnarled, thick leafless stems at their feet (whereas the young saplings are lush from their tips smack down to the ground), they're shorter and considerably thinner than their younger siblings.

My experience with wisteria was identical. The plants I bought in 15-gallon containers so that I could immediately tie their long tendrils to the top of their appointed pergola are now far less handsome than the tiny plants I placed at less strategic points (some of the older ones are smaller now, too).

The key to growing most perennials, trees, and shrubs to perfection is beginning with a root system that can comfortably support the growth above it. The larger the plant, the more massive its roots, and further growth won't budge until roots say it's okay. While waiting for roots to catch up, plants merely piddle around. Roses live by identical rules.

I've been thought ungrateful when refusing to accept certain rosebushes for my garden. "Why, it must be twenty years old," people have bragged about a mature shrub of the fine Gallica rose 'Madame Hardy'. "You're welcome to the whole thing."

I don't want the whole thing. Hefty mature rosebushes are a terror to transplant, and without the help of a sturdy back, an even sturdier backhoe, and several sacks of strong burlap, you'll never move an intact root ball no matter how careful you are. An alternative, of course, is to prune the bush severely and hope that the roots you drag along are adequate to get the plant going again. Take my word, if you can get your hands on a young Grade 1 bareroot bush, plant it instead. In three years, you won't be able to tell the difference between it and a twenty-year-old specimen (unless, of course, the transplanted specimen is still waiting for its roots to take hold, in which case it will pale in comparison to junior).

When gardeners move to a new home without a garden, they ache to start one, and nothing beats a few specimen plants to serve as focal points. Thankfully, certain plants *should* be purchased after they mature. Japanese maples, for instance, are praised for the curious shapes they assume with age. Buy one with a figure that appeals to you from the get go. *Magnolia Campbellii* can take up to twenty-five years to bloom. Who cares to wait that long? Rhododendron and azalea not only transplant well as adults, they happily do so in full bloom, assuring that gardeners don't pamper a mislabeled plant that flowers the wrong color.

If you visit my garden, be sure to notice the bay hedge. The trees with awkward feet are the ones for which I foolishly paid a fortune.

I could kick myself—that landscape architect, too.

Hasty Choices, Weighty Regrets

~ ∽

P eople who've been aching for a garden of their own often plant without regard to the future. A friend of mine bought a home on the San Francisco peninsula that was in need of remodeling. One of the reasons he purchased the fixer-upper was that it had a large, sunny rear lot that he ached to claim as his hobby. Because the house demanded attention first, he put his landscaping dreams on hold.

One sunny spring day, weary of carpentry and eagerly anticipating horticulture, he visited his local nursery. As it happened, magnolias were on special. My friend wasn't certain of all the plants he would ultimately include in his garden, but of one thing he was sure: He had to have a magnolia tree to refresh those scented memories of his youth.

He told the nursery employee that he wanted a fragrant white variety with thick petals. The employee suggested *Magnolia grandiflora,* which sounded precisely like what my friend had in mind, especially the *grand* part. He rushed home, dug a hole smack dab in the middle of his rear yard, and planted the magnolia.

A year later, when he could finally turn his attention to serious gardening, a landscape consultant shocked my friend by telling him that the first alteration his garden would need was transplanting that magnolia to the rear edge of the lot. "Are you crazy?" my friend asked. "That tree couldn't be happier anywhere else. Why, it's doubled in size since I planted it." "That's just the problem," the consultant replied. "By the time it's done with its doublings, it will be more than 60 feet tall and branch out over the entire garden, meaning that you can grow only shade lovers underneath."

My friend agonized over uprooting the magnolia for a month before he took out his shovel and set about doing what he knew was inevitable. (That magnolia tree is now more than 70 feet tall and spreads its branches over neighbors' yards in two directions.)

Uprooting stories like this one abound in the world of gardening and every eager newcomer who's made a similar mistake will advise you to go easy on woody plants, especially trees. It's not simply a matter of many woody plants becoming too large, it's also the agony of ripping them out from planting sites that suit them perfectly.

According to the late Henry Mitchell, the fine gardening columnist for *The Washington Post,* "There is no such thing as laying out a garden from scratch that will look all right in three years and also look all right in fifteen years." Gardening is a continuing process of digging out and chopping down. Mitchell's advice: Think clearly about plants you want forever and then plant them so that no matter what else comes and goes, they will have space to develop.

This doesn't mean that if you have your heart set on magnolia the way my friend did, you can't have a moderately sized tree, nor should you be denied a privet hedge, as long as you don't buy *Ligustrum lucidum* (actually an evergreen tree!).

Similarly, if you have a hankering for David Austin's English roses, have them, just steer clear of giants such as 'Leander' and 'Yellow Charles Austin'. Or, if you yearn for rhododendron, but can't afford much space in front of that picture window, don't plant 'Cornubia', which won't rest until it's at least 7 feet tall and the only plant in view. Plant the new diminutive form of 'Fragrantissimum' instead.

Before you dig a hole to accommodate the roots of a woody plant, make certain you see for yourself (as close to home as possible) what it will look like at maturity. Maybe your garden can't handle it.

Go Ahead, Break
That Rule

∽

"R oses must have at least six hours of direct sunlight every day. Never plant rosebushes where you would plant ferns." For the first twenty years I grew roses, I sounded like a broken record, and grew increasingly impatient with people who asked which roses liked growing in shade. "No roses like shade," I snapped back. "Plant azalea and rhododendron."

I was wrong.

My rosebushes are planted in an open field where 90 percent of them get sunlight from daybreak until sunset; the remaining 10 percent are shaded in late afternoon by a bank of native California willow trees. Although I resented the shade the flimsy willows cast, I admired the sturdy wind protection they afforded.

Not many years after growing roses in this idyllic sunny state, I began noticing that those roses protected from late-afternoon sunlight were sometimes more intensely colored and longer stemmed than those from bushes basking in full sun. Could roses flourish in even less sun?

I decided to experiment. Besides, that grove of tedious-green native willows was beginning to bore me. I didn't dare remove them, but they needed dressing up. Could roses possibly prosper in their dense shade?

In order to improve my chances for success, I began with roses I thought most likely to accept shade, specifically two members of the *Rosa chinensis* family. First, I decided to give that hell-bent-for-survival, bright midpink 'Old Blush' a try. 'Old Blush' is commonly known as one of the four stud roses kidnapped from China in the late eighteenth century because of its enviable habit of blossoming throughout summer rather than just in late spring, the way most old garden roses do. (These roses were called stud roses because their pollen proved exceptionally potent for crossbreeding.)

Next, I settled on 'Gold of Ophir', another China rose. Although I appreciated the heritage of this rose (also known as 'Fortune's Double Yellow', in honor of the man who discovered it growing in a Mandarin's garden), secretly, I chose 'Gold of Ophir' because it was M. F. K. Fisher's favorite climbing rose, and I liked pleasing Mary Frances. Finally, I also realized that if I could coerce 'Gold of Ophir' to grow in the shade, its blossoms would light up those willows. Blooms of this fine heirloom climber are a dazzling blend of shades of red and yellow that Mary Frances said look like "a moon on fire."

This story has a happy ending, but it took a while to reach. The first two years these plants were in the ground, they were spindly and doled out meager blossoms. Then they hit their stride during the third year and vigorously craned their necks toward the sun. By the time the arching branches reached the tops of the willows, they went bananas and now blossom as outrageously as their siblings growing on a pergola in full sun.

Gardeners break other garden rules because they're forced to. During California's recent drought, for instance, gardeners from Eureka to San Diego learned that supposed water lovers such as camellias, viburnums, forsythias, and lilacs survived with no evidence of neglect on a fraction of the water they previously enjoyed. "We were probably overwatering all along," gardeners admit.

I've noticed that gardeners who break supposedly cardinal garden rules are so highly motivated to achieve, that they inevitably do. Foxgloves, for instance, will tolerate full sun if kept moist, and a host of plants known to be fussy over drainage will behave if you go to the trouble of planting in raised beds.

Before you get carried away with shady roses, however, remember that you must choose varieties carefully. Start with a climber or a tough shrub like a Rugosa. *Never* plant a Hybrid Tea in the shade—it won't budge.

It Was a Flop—
Get Over It

W hen I began gardening, I considered it a sacrilege to remove any plant that I made grow. Later, as my addiction to horticulture grew beyond the limits of my land, I rethought garden tenancy rules and decided that just because certain plants flourished there, they had no right to call my garden home.

For instance, strictly because of its famous, fat, decadently fragrant, apricot blossoms, 'Helen Traubel' was one of the first Hybrid Tea roses I planted. The blooms lived up to their reputation and I soon coveted them indoors. My greed was so voracious that it blinded me to Helen's deadly flaw—a weak neck.

The blossoms of this dowager rose are huge, requiring strong stems to hold them erect. Alas, Madam Traubel's stems are so spindly that mature blooms persistently nod. Once I learned that the blossoms of 'Just Joey' are just as large and every bit as fragrant as those of 'Helen Traubel' and held straight up besides, I gave Helen the heave-ho.

When it comes to proper handling of poor garden performers, I side with Vita Sackville-West, the famous garden trendsetter from County Kent, England. If a rose, or any garden plant for that matter, doesn't perform well, she said, get rid of it. Replace it with something that has either already proven itself or shows all likelihood of it.

Roses deserve a two-year test. I have grown varieties that performed poorly the first year, then lived up to my expectations the second year and thereafter. But I have never grown a rose that took longer than two years to get me to like it—if I was ever going to. After two years, bushes that don't make the grade should be pruned with a shovel.

My biggest mistake in the herb patch was planting mint. Because of mint's notorious invasive habits, I had been advised to plant it in pots sunk in the ground rather than in open beds—good advice, but not good enough. While binding mint's roots in a pot helps, it won't keep mint from spreading; you must constantly be on the prowl for runners that reach out from their containers and greedily root themselves in soil intended for other plants. When mint overtook my herb garden, I yanked it, vowing never again to plant mint near any other herb.

Fortunately, mistakes with mint are easily corrected because, unlike most herbs, mint prefers semishade to full sun and moderately rich soil. Look for carefree areas near the back of the garden, such as where tall willowy trees grow. There, mint makes a comely, albeit tall, ground cover. Promise to weed out any runners that root themselves out of bounds of allocated space. Finally, to make certain that you plant the precise scent your nose dictates, plant mint from runners, not seeds, which rarely germinate true to parentage.

Certain members of the perennial border are mistakes in waiting, especially those plants that forget they're supposed to rebloom from mother plants year after year, rather than liberally reseeding themselves. If seedlings of *Oenothera Berlandieri* (commonly known as Mexican evening primrose), for instance, have their way, they'll choke a bed of mixed annuals in three years. Give away three quarters of volunteer seedlings every late spring.

Offering them as presents is a dandy solution for easing out of mistakes in the garden. Besides those seedlings of Mexican evening primrose, I give pots of mint to friends, advising them to keep the plants right there—in the pot.

I even found a home for that bush of 'Helen Traubel'. A neighbor keeps bud vases of roses on a tall kitchen shelf and likes varieties whose blooms nod to her. She and Helen were meant for each other.

Little p, Big H

I heard about pH long before I knew what it meant. "Oh, I grow mostly camellias," savvy gardeners would say, "my soil is acidic, you know," whispering as if confessing to having a dispeptic stomach.

Although I realized that I should memorize the pH of my own soil, I dragged my feet. I grew only roses then and knew that rosebushes require only average soil under a blanket of nutritional mulch. Besides, I secretly feared that exposing my soil's pH meant that I would have to do something about it—more than I was prepared to bargain for.

Later, when I branched out from roses and was forced to read up on those plants I yearned to cultivate, I found that I couldn't escape pH—it was everywhere I read. "Lower this, increase that," references would tell me. Once I started paying attention, I discovered that pH isn't nearly so mysterious as it seemed.

The pH scale runs from 0 to 14 to distinguish the relative degrees of acidity or alkalinity of a soil. The lower the pH, the more acidic the soil; high numbers signify alkaline conditions. Soils with a pH of 7 are neutral and precisely where most agricultural crops would like to grow. Plants that blossom, however, are finicky about the pH of the soil in which they're expected to flower.

Rhododendron, for instance, likes acidic soils, but only to a point. If pH drops below 5, plants will vegetate beautifully but won't blossom. Rhododendron in soils with a pH higher than 7 will bloom, but flowers will be stunted or aborted before maturity. On the other hand, lavender (or any other plant native to the Mediterranean) won't budge unless soil is alkaline.

When I first decided to get acquainted with my soil's pH, I thought I should test it myself. I bought two kits—one with a tiny gauge and another with fibrous papers on which I spooned bits of moist soil, then watched for color clues. I got different gauge readings every time I sampled the same soil and my test papers never turned identical colors.

I turned to the Yellow Pages. Experts who test soil samples are listed under *Laboratories, Testing*. When requested, they send foolproof instructions for collecting samples. To get an idea of a garden's overall pH, soil is gathered from several sites then mixed inside a plastic bag and mailed for testing.

Reports from soil laboratories don't merely assign numerical pH values, they tell you what to do about them, depending upon what you care to grow. If, for instance, a soil sample comes from an area where you intend to plant acid lovers like azaleas or hostas, you might be told to add soil sulfur. On the contrary, if you yearn for herbs, your soil will likely need an alkaline punch from limestone.

Besides revealing pH, soil analyses tell about soil salinity (whether you're under- or overfertilizing), soil fertility (whether or not nutrients are available), and how to correct any deficiencies. If you fertilize with an irrigation system, a soil report taken from several areas will reveal whether your garden is being watered evenly or only in pinpoint spots.

Gardeners restricted to container plants need soil tests, too, especially if their passion for a particular plant has grown to exclusivity. Addicts with kitchens turned over to African violets or solariums dedicated to bromeliads relish sleeping well at night, knowing that their treasures are thriving in soil proper in pH.

Someone asked me recently about pH and I launched into my personal narrative of the pH scale.

"Oh, no," he said, "I know what it means, but what do the letters stand for?" I was fairly certain that *H* stood for *hydrogen,* but what about *p*—*probable?*

Now, I'm assured by the pros, *H* indeed stands for *hydrogen,* but *p* is an arbitrary letter assigned to mean *negative logarithm of,* so *pH* stands for the negative logarithm of hydrogen ion concentration in a single sample of soil.

I'm sorry I asked.

The Hush-Hush
C Word

∞

There comes a time in every gardener's life when he or she must take a stand where chemicals are concerned. Nowadays, garden chemicals have developed such a nasty reputation that many gardeners won't even discuss them. "I refuse to consider using sprays that kill helpful insects like the ladybugs and praying mantises that I hope will visit my garden," they say adamantly. "I'll just keep up my spray program with agricultural soap, thank you."

Three years ago, I lost to spider mites a mature *Styrax japonica* and two standards of laburnum. The reason I let those creepy microscopic mites get the upper hand is that their hosts grow near my vegetable garden, where I permit no pesticides. Although I remain politically correct whenever possible, I've bent my rules in the garden. I have no intention of handing over my delicious vegetables to any insect with a terminal case of the munchies.

Before you, too, banish the C word from your gardening vocabulary, be certain you fully understand the warnings printed on the labels of chemical sprays. If directions are followed to the letter, many products aren't nearly as dangerous as you may imagine.

As part of their pesticide registration regulations, most states require manufacturers of chemical materials to clearly label their products in one of three toxicity categories, depending on their LD50—a term you must understand if you have any intention of employing garden chemicals. LD50, usually listed as oral (amount that must be swallowed) but sometimes quoted as dermal (absorbed by the skin), is an expression of the lethal dose in milligrams, per kilogram of body weight, that kills 50 percent of laboratory test animals.

Chemicals with an LD50 between 0 and 50 make up toxicity Category I, with labels marked *danger* or *poison* (usually accompanied with a skull and crossbones). I believe these chemicals have no place in the garden, ever.

Toxic chemicals in Category II have an LD50 somewhere between 50 and 499 and are considered moderately toxic, hence the word *warning* on the label. The probable lethal dose for a 150-pound man is between 1 teaspoon and 1 ounce.

Chemicals in Category III have *caution* printed on their labels because LD50 rates between 500 and 4,999 mean that the average man's oral lethal dose is between 1 ounce and 1 pint.

To gain perspective on the relative toxicity of common items, you should know some LD50 ratings (the lower the LD50, the more toxic the chemical). Nicotine is 53;

caffeine, 192; aspirin, 1,240; and table salt is 3,320. Understand also that the probable lethal dosages of garden chemicals refer only to concentrations of the active ingredient of the product, not the commercially available diluted form—to croak, you'd have to drink even more of that. Still, you don't want even a headache, so if you decide to admit moderate- to low-toxicity chemicals to your garden, take precautions.

First, to avoid any possibility of irritation, cover all body parts and wear goggles and rubber gloves, even when mixing spray materials. Never use a solution stronger than the manufacturer suggests; don't remove chemicals from their labeled containers; and keep materials stored far from any child's reach.

When you must spray, use the safest material for the job. I used to rely on agricultural soaps, but found they were effective for only three to four days and left an unappealing soapy residue. Then I found a water-based miticide with an LD50 rating of 5,150 (almost nontoxic) that destroys diabrotica—those nasty gnawing insects that look like green ladybugs but are anything but beneficial.

I heard recently about parents who sued a school district because their children got headaches after lying on the lawn that the gardener had sprayed with glyphosate (known commercially as Roundup). As it happens, Roundup has an LD50 rating of 4,320, placing it near the almost non-toxic category (also making it safer than table salt, aspirin, or caffeine). I don't know how soon after the gardener sprayed that the children lied on the grass, or the vigor of their romp, or whether they had the cafeteria's saltshaker with them. Still, I suspect the allegation will amount to another bad rap for gardening's C word.

Delicious Garden Punch

W hen I visit nurseries in spring to buy fertilizer, I often find empty shelves. "We can't keep nutrients in store," nursery staff complains. Then, when I return to these same nurseries in summer, fertilizers of every conceivable strength are on sale.

I think what happens is that, starved for flowers in early spring, gardeners scramble to feed. Rewards for such nurturing are reaped in summer, of course, but then we slump into false complacency, pretending that plants will blossom nonstop until Mother Nature pelts cold rain on their parade. Not so; flowers with long blooming cycles require a steady supply of food if they're expected to extend their season.

Industry is somewhat to blame for our smugness because it taught us how to utilize slow release fertilizers—wonder-workers like Osmocote plant food, which is to gardening what Contac pills are to a cold. These tiny granules don't do all their work at once because they're incapsulated with coverings of different density that break down over time, depending on the warmth of the soil. I not only use these extenders, I bless them, but I've long since learned that their duty is done by August, the month I flood my garden with summer punch.

Whenever possible, I use organics because they're eternally safe. Besides, I like what organic fertilizers do to the structure of garden loam. Organics are natural stimulants like compost, manure, and fish emulsion. The more aged, the quicker they break down, making nutrients immediately available to hungry plants.

Because I live near a mushroom farm, I buy truckloads of mushroom compost (the medium in which mushrooms grow is good for only one crop, after which it's spent for mushroom production but pure gold to the garden). I also use aged manures, especially chicken and turkey because they're higher in nitrogen than steer manure. Aging, however, is key, since fresh manure burns roots, most quickly those treasured feeder roots that lie just below the soil's surface (also, green manure reeks the way you probably don't want your garden to smell).

When people ask me how much fish emulsion to apply, I assure them the sky's the limit. Fish emulsion is so gentle on plants that, if properly diluted (please avert your nose), it's virtually incapable of burning. If you intend to keep your hungry roses blooming from fish emulsion only, however, you better plan to rig up an IV feeding station at each bush.

When organics won't do the job, I'm among those gardeners who resort to chemicals. Chemical fertilizers have developed a nasty reputation in horticulture. That's a pity, because chemicals aren't nearly so dangerous as the people who use them without reading clearly printed labels.

The reason chemical fertilizers are problematic is that they're loaded with salts—sulfates like ammonium and calcium. Unless dosed along with a deep drink of water, these sulfates are sure to burn (once absorbed, plants have no depository for salts other than foliage). If you worry that your garden is in danger of salt burn, water whether your plants look like they need it or not, so sulfates sink deep in the ground, where they belong.

Fertilizers always have three numbers associated with them that reveal how much nitrogen, phosphorus, and potash they contain (always in that order). Nitrogen is a growth stimulant; potassium encourages bloom; and potash works leftover miracles, including color improvement. If a fertilizer is marketed as 20-10-10, that means that there is twice as much nitrogen as potassium or potash. Well-balanced fertilizers are those where the three elements are equal, like 20-20-20—my pick for summer punch.

I was recently told about a trick for making certain that dry fertilizers won't burn. Rather than spreading granules around the entire base of a plant, put a single glob off to one side. Research has proven that whole plants flourish from a single well-fed root. Should dry fertilizers still worry you, use liquids. Or, remulch, but feed *something;* spring's banquet is merely your garden's memory of its last decent meal.

Honing a Vegetable Garden

∽

Gardeners make more mistakes in the vegetable garden than anywhere else. I've been at it for thirty years. My first mistakes were the most obvious—overplanting. When I first moved to California, I fell in love with zucchini and imagined I couldn't grow enough of it. I built raised beds, double dug the soil, and strategically installed eight plants. By midsummer's bounty, friends avoided me; by August, I never wanted to see another zucchini. I've never since grown more than two plants at a time.

Similarly, I once devoted half my vegetable garden to corn and lived to regret it. Another year, I simply had more tomatoes than my neighbors or I needed, and I once cornered the market on perfectly shaped heads of radicchio.

Because I adamantly use no pesticide in my vegetable garden, I've parted company with certain homegrown vegetables—cabbage, broccoli, brussels sprouts, and cauliflower, for instance, because they all fall prey to the ravages of disgusting insects. Aphids are the worst, of course, but cabbageworms are a close second. Once I became environmentally correct, I began buying cabbages and their cousins at my local farmers' market.

Thanks also to these growers, I no longer plant peppers, chiles, potatoes, radishes, or spinach. Besides the space they take up, I really can't improve on the quality of those grown by farmers nearby.

Except for basil (which comes in an amazing array of flavors from lemon to cinnamon), I grow few herbs with my vegetables, planting them instead near other fragrant plants all around the garden (a plus when it comes to scraggly herbs such as tarragon, because companion plants provide support for lanky growth). Otherwise, the collection of vegetables I grow is vaguely narrow, but decidedly suited to my kitchen.

First, tomatoes, lots of tomatoes. I know that only six tomato plants will feed the average family, but my love of tomatoes isn't average. I plant very early, early, and mid-season varieties, as well as cherry and Italian plum tomatoes.

I also grow more beans than the average gardener. They are excellent sources of vitamins A and C, and are good for the garden, too, because they're "nitrogen fixers" (after harvest, bean plants leave enriching nitrogen-fixing bacteria in the soil where they grew). I plant pole beans not simply because they bear sweet slender beans, but also because many grow into handsome vines, 'Blue Lake', for instance. I also grow shelling beans, and always include the Italian favorite 'Borlotto', which bears pods stippled in rosy red and cream. This past year, I grew fava beans for the first time and will never be without them again. Besides being delicious on their own (particularly when immature), fava beans are a sensational addition to risotto.

Beans make zucchini look stingy; if you plant them, you must stagger bean crops. Always sow fewer than you think you'll need, spacing plantings by three-week intervals, and don't rely on memory. Mark your calendar and promise to replant on that date whether or not you feel like it.

Remember to stagger when planting another garden mainstay—lettuce. I plant romaine, butterhead, and bibb lettuce every three weeks for three months (arugula and mesclum by the same schedule).

I grow beets, but only golden and striped Italian varieties with cherry-red and creamy-white bands; eggplant and baby carrots or varieties suitable for harvesting as succulent fingerlings; leeks, a kitchen staple; Italian parsley (the curly varieties from the supermarket are just as good); and Petis Pois peas.

I've found a dandy solution for not growing my own corn. A friend who grows corn commercially is gaga over roses. We have a great deal going.

The Perils of Gardening
for a Living

ourteen years ago, when I started growing garden roses for the sale of their blooms, friends thought I had lost my mind. "Growing roses in your garden is one thing," they said, shaking their heads, "but growing outdoor roses as a business is much too risky a proposition."

But there was no use talking to me. I was incurably rose struck and I would have my rose ranch, risky or not.

Now that the commercial rose madness is a hit, those same doubtful friends act as though it was their idea. Occasionally, however, I've thought that they were right the first time.

Two years after the rose project began, my roses suffered a hideous infestation of downy mildew. Although the disease was well known (it's blamed for Ireland's 1848 potato blight), it hadn't been reported in California since 1906. Having never seen the disfiguring purple lesions that downy mildew causes, I had no idea what was going on with my roses, but for one whole week I thought I was going to lose every rosebush that I had cultivated.

Then, help came in the form of local agricultural agents who not only explained to me what caused the problem (periods of torrential rain followed by periods of unseasonable heat), but also how to eradicate it (spraying with a solution of fixed copper, not unlike the Bordeaux mixture my grape-growing neighbors use).

We didn't supply the floral trade with roses for Mother's Day that year, but by the end of May, the roses recovered well enough to stage a banner Memorial Day weekend. As if to make up for a slow start to the season, they bloomed until the week before Thanksgiving.

We missed Mother's Day again this year, not because of downy mildew, but rather because of a sudden infestation of thrips. We'd dealt with thrips before, of course, but never so many so suddenly. Literally overnight, a swarm of the nasty microscopic insects dropped down on the rose field in a giant swarm. They began their mighty munch with their favorites—whites and pale pinks—but in slightly more than one day, moved on to stronger colors. We ended up composting every rose the thrips infested.

Between these two Mother's Day misses, other nasty problems cropped up. The bummer summer we had three years ago brought mornings so wet that it was all we could do to stay ahead of botrytis. In viticulture, botrytis is known as the noble rot because it's what makes the difference between mediocre and sensational sauternes. But in rose-dom, botrytis is anything but noble. If rain or heavy dew creeps in between rose petals of blossoms as they open, it festers and turns petals an unappealing brown. Once present in a bloom, botrytis continues to develop until it rots the base of all petals.

Recently I've been told that the reason my Grandiflora rose 'Gold Medal' is dropping its leaves is because it has "alternia," a fungal infection known only to this variety. There is no cure, "but it will disappear by fall." Thanks a lot.

Other floriculturists have their problems, too. A friend who grows fuchsias told me about a weird mite unintentionally imported from Brazil that is airborne (often carried by hummingbirds) and horribly disfiguring to blooms, but has no known predators. A woman who grows orchids professionally lives in fear of orchid scale, which starts out as pale waxy scales that are practically unnoticeable until whole plants are encrusted. An acquaintance devoted to chrysanthemum worries about gall midge, a mum predator that leaves unattractive pitted marks on petals and foliage.

So seemingly at odds with Mother Nature, you'd think we'd give up horticultural pursuits for an office job, wouldn't you? Never.

Plants Need a Good Talking To

A friend who is a terrific rosarian and a formidable exhibitor told me that he finally scared his bush of the aggravating Hybrid Tea rose 'Royal Highness' into shaping up.

"Her Highness pouted if a cloud passed overhead," my friend lamented. "One day, I said: 'Look, Missy, either shape up or its compostville for you.' "

My rose buddy swears that his message rang through because at the very next rose convention, he won Queen of the Show (the highest honor paid to a single-stemmed rose in competition) with the finicky 'Royal Highness'.

Since it feels so natural, I can't imagine why nongardeners have such difficulty understanding why those of us who love plants talk to them. First, an undeniable benefit—carbon dioxide. Plants thrive on the absorption of carbon dioxide, and when humans speak, they exhale it. Second, if we're expected to believe what passes for horticultural research, the literature abounds with reports of how much better corn crops behave when overhead speakers play opera and how fields of delphiniums demonstrate preferences for Verdi.

The very best reason for communicating with plants, however, is that talking forces you to look at them, during which time you may spot what's keeping them from the performance of your dreams. If, for instance, a plant is suffering from an infestation of aphids, the only way to know that is so see the nasty critters yourself, and they're not always easy to spot because aphids are often the exact shade of green as the flower buds they're sucking dry. Similarly, spider mites (the dread of August) aren't visible to the naked eye; they're microscopic, but their ravages aren't. If you worry that mites are sinking tiny vicious bites into your treasures, examine the bottoms of plants for webs and lower leaves that look as though they're about to turn brown and die.

Plants sometimes suffer badly simply from a shortage of water. Tall plants signal impending deprivation with limp foliar growth on top. If, while speaking to thirsty plants, you notice lifeless young growth, scratch around the base of each plant and give it a good drink when it feels dry.

Foliage often tells what whole plants are going through. When leaves that are supposed to be dark green aren't, consider that the plant on which they grow is deficient, say, in iron or nitrogen. Plants needing greening up often appear healthy overall, but individual leaves look sickly. When a spray of iron chelate is what the doctor orders, matters turn from lime to emerald green in a couple of days.

While talking to plants that seem unhappy, stay on the lookout for suckers—those vigorous growths that stem not from the hybrid you intend to cultivate, but rather from the rootstock onto which it's budded. Suckers differ from their host plant not only in the color of their blossoms, but also in the formation of their foliage, but they all rob nourishment. Cut them out.

Trees and shrubs that must be staked need a good talking to occasionally, especially tall ones that require ties at various heights. Materials used to tie skyscrapers to their stakes shouldn't become girdled in growth. Relieve them.

Gardeners restricted to sundecks and container plants must speak with their plants, too, in order to notice if they need repotting because their cramped roots mound at ground level, need rotating because all growth is aimed in one direction, or are languishing in saucers of stale water.

Don't simply converse with plants in trouble; praise those performing well, too. When a plant drives your patience to the limit, threaten it. After all, if a rose as vexing as 'Royal Highness' responds, anything else is bound to.

PART 2

Gardening
Tips

Methuselah's Favorite Flowers

∽

My friend Joan called in a panic late last February. "I don't know why I agreed to do this silly thing, but it seemed like a good idea at the time," she said in an exasperated tone. "Last July, I told a search committee that I'd enter an arrangement in their winter floral show. I just came back from casing out the flower market—it looks like Holland, and I don't want responsibility for yet another mass of tulips and daffodils."

Although I ached to ask what else she fantasized last July, I told her instead that she could have anything from my garden, but that pickings were slim. Joan fell in love on sight with the notorious harbinger of spring *Magnolia stellata*—both its fanciful flowers and its intricately twisted branches. "How long will the blossoms last?" she asked, concerned because the arrangement had to hold up for three days. I told her I didn't know, that I had never tried that particular magnolia as a cut flower.

The day before the show, we cut armloads of star magnolia in tight fat buds and smashed the end of their stems in hopes of improving water and preservative absorption. I told Joan to leave the bucket of magnolias in her basement where it's cool and not to touch them until she got to the show. I considered calling my friend the evening after the show opened, but decided that such action would make me sound like the kind of consort who'd be insulted if she didn't win. Three days later, I received a card.

"I did just what you told me," she began, then went on to explain that even though her basement was cool and dark, most of the buds opened before morning; worse yet, blossoms dropped their petals on the way to the show. "I ended up with tulips and daffodils, after all," she lamented.

After Joan's fiasco, I asked a florist friend if he ever used star magnolia in arrangements. "Only if someone walks behind me with a Hoover," he answered.

If you grow or buy flowers to enjoy indoors, you should know what does and doesn't last in a vase. First, the biggies. It's hard to beat the lasting power of orchids; some varieties hold up even out of water. Although I find most chrysanthemums more serviceable than appealing, I've got to hand it to them—they last an eternity. Even after being away from the south for three decades, I still think of funerals when I see gladioli—another dud with staying power.

Flowers with an intermediate vase life (usually one week) include gerberas, lilies, asters (particularly American asters and especially ones with yellow centers), freesias, hydrangeas (darker colors last longest), mullein, tulips (cottage and Darwins outlive parrots and doubles), and flowering herbs such as dill, oregano, and lavender.

Blossoms that flower atop willowy weedy stems such as forget-me-nots, delphiniums, and gauras should be thought of as two-dayers; they don't draw water well or retain preservatives.

Be careful, too, with flowers whose stems exude viscous saps. For instance, don't mix daffodils with tulips if you want your arrangement to last. The sap that daffodils ooze will clog the tips of the tulip stems and shorten their life spans. Calla lilies are oozers also, but they pale in comparison to stock, which makes whole vases look and smell like yuck.

All flowers benefit from having their stems periodically recut. Unless a few drops of bleach have been added to vase water, bacteria forms rapidly and clogs stem tips. Removing the blockage with sharp shears gives stems a clear route to a fresh drink.

As Joan will ruefully attest, no manner of doting will extend the life of the *Magnolia stellata* blossom, however. Better leave it on the tree.

Extending Vase Life

A gardening pal called recently to report that after following all of my suggestions for growing knockout roses, she was sickened to see her pretty blossoms nod in their vases only two days after she cut them. "Where do you suppose I went wrong?" she asked in a voice quivering from heartache.

After answering satisfactorily all of my nagging questions about good rose culture, I asked how she harvested her blooms. She assured me she was careful there, too; she took a bucket of cold water with her into the garden and plunged her roses inside as soon as she snipped them from their bushes. "Well, there's your problem," I assured her, "you must start cutting stems under water."

"Do what?" she asked incredulously. I had dealt with this shocked response before. When I tell people about the necessity of cutting stems under water, they act as though I've ordered them to submerge their flowers (and themselves) into a tub of water, and, without benefit of goggles, slice bouquets into smithereens.

I explained to my friend that by taking a bucket of water with her into the garden, she was inevitably bound to either slosh water on her feet or wrench her back. Rather than risking either of these horrors, I convinced her to cut roses from her bushes and to lay one stem carefully over another in her favorite wicker basket. Next, I suggested that she take her bounty into her kitchen, fill a bowl with fresh water, submerge the tips of each stem one or two inches under water, and, with the help of the same sharp shears she used to cut the roses, recut ¼ inch from the bottom of each stem. Then, each rose could be placed in a bud vase or mixed into an arrangement.

When roses, lilacs, daphnes, magnolias, acacias, rhodo-dendrons, azaleas, and a host of other pithy-stemmed flowers are cut from their bushes, they draw in air and begin to make pockets, which, when they reach the bloom, cause the blossom to nod in premature death. When stems are recut under water, they draw no air, and the water acts as a temporary sealant when blossoms are later moved around out of water.

If you want to truly gild the lily and enjoy the longest vase life possible, you should learn about two trade secrets that florists call "conditioning and hardening." They couldn't be much easier, involving only preservatives and hot water. You probably already know about conditioning (the use of preservatives), having utilized the concoctions housed in soft plastic bags stapled to floral bouquets. Hardening is nothing more than placing cut blossoms in hot water to which preservatives have been added and leaving them there until the water reaches room temperature. In practical terms for properly conditioning roses and other pithy-stemmed flowers, here's how the data translates to the longest possible vase life. Before cutting, mix preservatives with 105° F. water (usually the hottest water you can get from a kitchen tap). Newly cut flowers quickly absorb preservatives if there's a good drink of warm water to go with them. After you cut roses from the garden, under water, recut ¼ inch off their stems and put them in a container with hot water (stems absorb hot water more quickly than cold) to which bleach (household bleach works perfectly well) has been added (½ ounce per 8 gallons, or ⅟₆₄ ounce—two to three drops—per quart). In the darkest, coolest spot you can find (ground-floor closets are ideal), store the container until the water comes to room temperature (preferably overnight). By the next morning, blooms will be turgid.

Then, recut stems under water again and arrange them in containers holding water fortified with ¾ teaspoon (per quart) of floral preservative and a couple of drops of bleach. I'm so sold on bleach that I use it with hollow-stemmed cut flowers, too. Can't hurt. You'll be happy you went to this tiny bit of extra trouble as the days go by and by and your precious blooms last and last.

Now that my friend has mastered these techniques, she calls me to tell about blossoms that lasted far longer than I suspect they really did. Even so, I don't challenge her. I, too, exaggerated when I first learned how to extend vase life.

How to Retire a Garden Hose Properly

❧

B ack when I was sane and grew only 100 rosebushes, my favorite chore was watering with a garden hose fitted with a water wand that whooshed water out in gentle sprays. Hand-watering afforded a satisfying opportunity to take a good look at bushes and for deciding which blossoms to cut, after they enjoyed a stiff drink. Later, when my addiction to roses grew to the point that I was forced to go commercial and ended up with 8,000 rosebushes to coddle, I had no time to stand around with a hose.

I didn't even consider installing my first irrigation system myself, assuming instead that it was so complicated that only an expert could properly assemble it. That specialist taught me a lot about irrigation systems, including that I could install them myself. So can you, if you take the foolproof instructions handed out by the specialists the Yellow Pages call *irrigation suppliers*. All parts of modern irrigation systems are plastic and easily assembled with specially prepared tough fixative glues.

My first system was a flop—drip irragation. Although many gardeners sing the praises of a drip system, few of them are rosarians. Drip systems are wrong for rose growers for two reasons. First, emitters from drip systems often get clogged, and this isn't discovered until plants wither from thirst. With roses, that happens quickly. Second, rosebushes like to grow under a comfy carpet of mulch, not simply because it retains moisture and discourages weeds, but also because, when irrigated, mulch breaks down slowly over a growing season, releasing nutrients with each watering. The only way to take maximum advantage of mulch is to soak it thoroughly. Drip systems won't do the job because they release steady drops of water from a pinpoint spot, leaving whole patches of mulch parched.

In order to flood my rose beds, I next tried bubblers. Bubblers gurgle water from frothy mounds about the size of golf balls. My bubbling system certainly flooded my mulch, but it also displaced it in unsightly patterns with each irrigation.

My third system, microjet sprinkler heads, was a rousing success for two reasons. First, water was disbursed in an even pattern over the entire rose bed, soaking every shred of mulch in sight. Second, since the emitters were fitted atop 8-inch stems, they sprayed the bottom quarters of all rosebushes, thereby discouraging spider mites, the dread of August.

Before committing to any irrigation system, look closely at the plants you intend to water and determine the best way to irrigate them. Poplar trees, for instance, don't really care how they're watered as long as it's frequently. I moved those bubblers to the Lombardy poplars, which loved the action. Hedges of yew aren't particular over what's between them and the soil, nor are they fussy about how they're watered. The drip system that didn't work for my heavily mulched roses thrills the mulchless yews. Rhododendron and azalea like being watered overhead—a snap with water-emitting heads fitted atop threaded slender stems 2 to 6 feet tall.

As for lawns, I shudder to think of the times I've miscalculated how quickly I could dash past a rotating sprinkler fitted to a live garden hose. Ever since I learned that I could connect permanent pop-up sprinkling heads to the same PVC pipe I used for all other systems, I've stayed dry.

Today's home irrigation systems are so simple that you should imagine one long piece of ½- to ¾-inch flexible pipe snaking around your garden with water distribution heads set every few feet at varying heights (low here, high there, intermediate elsewhere), determined by each plant's preference.

You can still visit with your plants while they're drinking; you'll simply have two free hands for doing so yourself.

Comfy Mulch

E very gardener I know has a personal secret to good horticulture. Some confess it's watering plants only in the morning. "Never send plants to bed with wet feet," they say. Other gardeners swear by their fertilizer schedules. "Use a pat-on-the-back approach," these plant feeders claim, "and fertilize repeat bloomers with a shot of nitrogen just after they finish a flush of blossoms."

I say, combine the best of both worlds with a cozy blanket of mulch, the nutrients of which are released every time plants are watered, no matter what time. Although mulching is nothing more than layering organic material over soil, in all of garden culture, nothing is more practical or more beneficial to plants and the beds in which they grow.

Mulch makes three important contributions to plant culture. First, every time plants are irrigated, water flows over and through mulch, slowly releasing its nutrients. Mulch is organic and contains valuable ingredients that aren't available all at once, but break down steadily during growing seasons, usually reducing their bulk by half each year.

Second, mulch conserves water and provides a blanket of protection from the hard rays of summer sun. Because many garden plants like to be watered infrequently but deeply, mulch holds water under the soil surface and keeps it available between soakings.

Finally, thank goodness, mulching controls weeds. If mulch is thick enough, weeds can't poke through it; if they do, they're not difficult to remove because the soil under the mulch is friable and the roots of wispy weeds can't anchor themselves.

The mulch of choice depends on the plants expected to grow beneath it. Acid lovers such as azaleas, camellias, and rhododendrons are the easiest of all plants to mulch because they're already planted in the same wood by-products you mulch them with—shavings, rough bark, or compressed pellets the size of poker chips. Alkaline lovers (particularly those that like soil fortified with nitrogen) appreciate a variety of mulch materials. And no material is more important than manure. Although it is rich in nutrients, an even bigger plus is the heat it generates while decomposing, which warms soil and expedites bacterial reactions.

Make certain that any manure you choose is well aged. Fresh manure is hot and fatal to plants with tender feeder roots. Choose specific manures to satiate the appetite of the plants you cultivate. If you grow roses or other gluttons, the richer the better.

Chicken is the richest of fowl manures, with a nitrogen count of 1.5 percent (cage chickens are said to be richer than broilers). Turkey is a close second, especially if the manure hasn't been mixed with shavings or feathers.

Among animal manures, sheep is richest (1 percent nitrogen), followed by pig or horse (.6 percent) and cow (.5 percent). Accuracy compels me to mention that liquid sludge has a nitrogen count higher than all other sources of manure (2.5 percent), but I doubt if you want your garden to smell like a sewer.

Additional mulch materials can be anything organic that breaks down into humus—compost, aged bark, leaf mold, rice hulls, or peat moss. Sawdust and wood shavings are good sources for mulch bulk, but they require a source of nitrogen separate from that meant for plants to complete their own breakdown.

Look for special sources of mulch close to where you garden. If you live near a mushroom farm, for instance, buy its compost, which is good for only one crop of mushrooms but pure gold to other plants thereafter.

If you refuse to fuss with any of these mulches, at least rake up your grass clippings or pine needles and spread them around plants. Although these materials tend to mat and cause water runoff, even a crusty mulch is better than none at all.

How Long Have We
Been Planting Too Low?

⚭

T wo years ago, Bob Galyean planted an area of the garden we shared with ornamental grasses that took off
like gangbusters in our sandy riverbed soil. We knew we
were placing young plants too close together, but didn't
care to wait three years for the mature effect.

After growing only one season, the grasses were filling in
nicely, but certain varieties outperformed themselves. One
in particular, a stand of *Cortaderia Selloana* 'Gold Band', had
developed at lightning speed, and its plants were crowding
each other out. Early the next spring, Bob removed the
center plants from each stand of one-year-olds and set them
aside on bare ground. He intended to transplant the clumps
immediately, of course, but a more pressing garden chore
took precedence and he forgot all about them.

At the end of the second growing season, I noticed that
certain plants of our hell-bent-for-survival 'Gold Band'
grasses were taller than others. When Bob returned from
finding out why, he told me that the giants were those plants
he dug up and never properly replanted. "Mother Nature is

trying to tell us something," Bob said, "and I believe we should rethink the depth we're planting around here."

When I told this story to my friend Bonnie, she admitted to an identical experience. "I grow lots of sedum," she said, "and my 'Autumn Joy' were so delirious, they were spreading into a path. I dug some up to give away and tossed the leftovers behind my garden shed. Those orphans are now the biggest sedum in my garden."

Bob, Bonnie, and I have decided that certain plants clearly appreciate more oxygen than others. Our planting rule of thumb is: The more drought tolerant the plant, the higher above ground it should be planted.

Never apply our rule to plants known to be persistently thirsty. Ferns, for instance, will keel over in no time if their roots aren't planted well under moist soil, and clematis vines must have their root crown at least two inches underground.

The overall appearances of certain plants can fool you about how deep they like being planted. Lush lilac bushes, for instance, appreciate moist soil, but they want their roots to rise above it. Plant lilacs two inches higher than you think you should (unless, of course, you already knew this about lilac, in which case you also know to give them a dose of lime each spring).

Bushes and trees planted at the right level sometimes later sink to doom. Unfortunately, this happens to gardeners with the best of intentions—those who carefully prepare planting sites with compost, organic materials, and manures.

Alas, rich soil additives condense because the materials that make them rich are light (friable, in gardening lingo). If planted too soon, bushes and trees sink low enough to allow water to stand on their root crowns, which soon rot.

Not only should you never sink a nursery plant deeper into soil than it was in its container, you must never tamper with ground level once plants mature. I was told about new homeowners who decided that they'd like to enjoy the shade of their mature Douglas fir tree, and built a 2-foot container around its perimeter with a comfy ledge to sit on. The wooden frame was filled with soil and planted with cascading annuals. The tree died in a year.

The very best solution to deciding on planting depth is to plant on the high side and cover exposed roots with mulch, thereby achieving two highly desirable horticultural conditions: abundance of oxygen and retention of moisture. Besides, mulch controls weeds, which, as you already know, also like to grow high.

Stagger, Stagger, Stagger

Until six months ago, I had a bad gardening habit that really bugged me. In spring, overcome by the joys of soil warm enough to till, I overplanted. "Who ever heard of too much arugula or butterhead lettuce?" I'd ask myself as I tilled multiple rows, "or sweet peas, with their irresistible scent of vanilla?" Secretly, of course, I knew I was making a familiar mistake—bumper crops would surely follow. "I'll just give away the surplus," I reassured myself. And I did— to everyone I've ever met who appeared even vaguely fond of salads or remotely longing to sniff sweet peas. These recipients acted grateful, of course, but still I knew I was in error and that evenly paced crops would be preferable.

Then, a veterinarian informed me that, because my beloved dog Sadie, a German shorthair, not only patrols my rose ranch but also the adjoining dairy (munching lord knows what), she was in danger of developing heartworms. "Just give her one of these meat-flavored pills every four weeks. To help you remember when to dose," my friendly vet suggested, "here are some red heart-shaped stickers to affix to your wall calendar."

As it happened, Sadie's first medication was scheduled on the same day I was to plant lettuces. After making sure she swallowed her pill, I marched into the vegetable garden to scatter my seeds. By the time I had planted one third of the seeds from the first packet, I had already sown three rows. "That's enough romaine," I muttered, "but I might as well plant the rest." Just as I stretched my hand toward the fourth hill, the idea struck me. "Why not plant again in four weeks when I give Sadie her next pill?" I asked myself.

I'm a changed man. Now, I have lettuces at all stages—baby sprouts that must be thinned to make way for a mature crop, midsized leaves, and fully developed plants just on the brink of bolting. You can't imagine how my heart-shaped visual aid has improved my eating habits. I've grown beyond lettuce, of course, and now use the same technique for staggering beans and peas, even root crops like radishes and carrots.

Next year, I intend to stagger the crops in my cutting garden, too, since a host of flowers bloom over extended seasons if their seeds aren't planted all at once. Sweet peas head the list. Because there are already early-flowering, spring-flowering, and summer-flowering varieties, plus bush and knee-high strains, the additional assist of staggered plantings assures sweet peas year-round. Besides spacing plantings over time, it helps considerably if you vow to pick blossoms, since that's the ticket for keeping sweet peas in blossom (if you let up, vines assume you want them to go to seed).

Snapdragons and stock can also be planted for staggered crops, thereby assuring a steady supply of two of the best all-purpose cut flowers known to the garden. Similarly, linaria, which many people call baby snapdragons, can be kept in bloom from early summer until late fall if seeds aren't sown during a single planting, in which case plants peter out (especially if there's a greedy flower arranger with a pair of shears nearby).

Finally, I've pledged to extend the bloom of one of my favorite springtime annuals, *Nemophila Menziesii,* better known as baby-blue-eyes. This utterly charming California native that most people assume thrives only in the wilds is perfectly at home in gardens. Sky-blue, 1-inch cupped flowers with white eyes handsomely camouflage leftover foliage from spring bulbs and will blossom until early summer if seeds aren't scattered all at once.

Try granting yourself visual aids like stickers on a wall calendar to make certain you stagger crops. They certainly worked for me.

Sadie's fine, by the way, and still all heart.

Don't Let Pruning
Intimidate You

◞◟

Nothing about horticulture frightens novice gardeners more than pruning. "You expect me to cut it off *where*?" they ask incredulously when you assure them that artichoke plants should be hacked to the ground before each growing season. "Nothing will be left," they grumble.

Gardeners prune for two reasons: to eliminate nonproductive growth, thereby encouraging new growth; and to shape plants. Dormant bushes aren't certain which way you want them to grow unless you prune to budding eyes pointed in the right direction. Unless aimed correctly, wisteria doesn't know whether to scramble this way or that. Without an annual thinning, many plants become a thorny tangle with centers that never see the light of day.

On the other hand, some plants such as cistus bushes and eucalyptus trees can enjoy a whole lifetime untampered by shears. Inevitably, however, 99 percent of the perennial garden will eventually cry out to be pruned. If you intend to answer such cries for help, before taking the first judicious slice, arm yourself with proper pruning gear. Shears head the list. Skimp on any garden tool other than shears. The proper shears will not only see you through pruning, they'll stick by you for seasons of harvesting blooms. Good shears aren't cheap, but easily worth their price when you consider protecting the investment of an entire garden.

First, buy shears that can be sharpened, not those that "never need it," for they surely will. Next, keep shears well honed with the easy assist of an Arkansas sharpening stone and a can of all-purpose household oil. Shears should be comfortable to hold and easy to work. The one-hand hook and blade types I prefer are on the heavy side of average weight, but anything lighter seems flimsy.

Eventually, as your garden grows, so must pruning tools—loppers for rambunctious stems developed beyond the grasp of hand-pruners, and a keyhole saw for difficult-to-reach woody spurts of growth. In the beginning, however, and for 80 percent of the cuts required at maturity, most plants can be satisfactorily pruned with handheld shears.

Next, familiarize yourself with the months when certain plants want to be pruned and get ready for a calendar of preferences. Although most plants should be shorn just before a growing season (right after the threat of a hard frost has passed), others like acacia and forsythia can be cut while blooming.

Plants in large families are especially tricky because all members can't be treated equally. Unlike most daphne, *Daphne Mezereum* will skip a whole year of bloom if you dare take shears to it. Maple and apple trees appreciate pruning for shape during their early years and only thinning at maturity. Similarly, ash trees should be trimmed during their formative years to prevent weak crotches.

With roses, it's important to understand pruning requirements by variety. The stately 'Queen Elizabeth' rose, for instance, won't stand for being sheared as low as other rosebushes. When pruned like her sister Grandiflora roses, Her Majesty pouts the whole next summer until reaching the lofty height from which she prefers to thrust her lovely blossoms.

With many plants, pruning rules are easy: Cut to the ground. Acanthus (the plant after whose leaves the Corinthian capital was modeled), buddleia (the butterfly bush), and Romneya (matilija poppy), like to be lopped off at the ankles each year. Remember, too, that pruning season is the time for ridding the garden of plants that don't please you. Nothing is worse than fussing over a plant you resent.

When I first grew roses, I planted 'Sterling Silver'. After all, it was the first modern mauve Hybrid Tea and notorious for heady fragrance. Still, in spite of my kowtowing to its every fickle whimsy, my bushes of 'Sterling Silver' were puny, stingy with bloom, and covered in mildew. Then, I discovered 'Angel Face', the granddaughter of 'Sterling Silver'. Not only was 'Angel Face' every bit as sumptuously perfumed, her bushes were vigorous and she bloomed all summer long.

That was the year I pruned 'Sterling Silver' with a shovel.

British Rosarians
Hedge the Issue

⬲

E nglish horticulturists have let the cat out of the bag where rose pruning is concerned. Britain's Royal National Rose Society (RNRS) has just confessed to more than three years of experimentations with unconventional rose pruning techniques, including the use of pruning shears and hedge clippers on bareroot plants.

I didn't think much about the news when I first heard it because I pruned my miniature roses that way for years. I never told anyone I was doing it because I thought they'd think it just another sign of my ambivalence to minis (although I'll never love them, I admire the hell-bent-for-survival habits of miniature roses, including their no-nonsense attitudes when it comes to pruning).

Still, pruning with hedge clippers sounded like a winning argument for that endless stream of people I try to persuade to grow roses. I yearned for enthusiasm, but I couldn't bring myself to think of rosebushes as hedges. Besides, what if someone tried to prune my beloved 'Color Magic' that way? Because of its wondrously colored, decadently scented, dinner-plate-sized blossoms, 'Color Magic' is my favorite rose in spite of its thoroughly vexing ways. Unless pruned precisely where it feels like giving up wood in winter, 'Color Magic' misbehaves all summer.

Before you can appreciate the profundity of the seemingly lazy British claim to unconventional pruning techniques, you must understand that conventional pruning of rosebushes requires a careful search for budding eyes that not only harbor new growth but are also pointed in the right direction. Pruning rosebushes with shears and trimmers is conducted in total abandon of where eyes harbor.

British rosarians have test programs underway on Hybrid Teas and Floribundas (England doesn't embrace the Grandiflora category of roses), which compare traditional pruning methods with rough methods (all stems cut to the same horizontal height), using pruning shears and hedge trimmers. So far, results are a virtual toss-up, except that the rough method "seems to give better short-term results than traditional pruning."

In an article by RNRS secretary Ken Grapes, published in the August 1992 issue of *The American Rose,* the British researchers point out that traditional pruning methods (searching for swelling bud eyes and cutting just above them) have been favored because modern roses were for years plagued with dieback—the tendency for unproperly cut stems to die back to the place where a proper cut should have been made. Now, the researchers say, "rose breeding has come a long way and many modern varieties don't suffer badly from the effects of dieback because they are so much more vigorous." Further, their trial "showed that rough pruning and hedge trimmer pruning caused no more dieback than traditional pruning."

Leaving themselves the obvious out, the British experimenters go on to allow that "it is possible that roses that are roughly pruned may become overcrowded in the center and therefore more prone to diseases. Traditional pruning encourages the development of open-centered bushes. It may therefore be necessary to alternate between rough, or hedge trimmer, pruning and traditional pruning."

I'll say it will. What's more, I predict that shearing large rosebushes (especially those cultivated for their blooms) with trimmers will never replace pruning them by hand. Still, I'll listen to what the British have to say. In the meantime, however, although you may see me with hedge clippers near my beds of Miniature roses, you'll never catch me with power trimmers near my Hybrid Teas, Floribundas, or Grandifloras. Someday, who knows?

Skip Pruning?
Not Worth It

L ast winter, when Bob Galyean and I finished overseeing the pruning of several thousand modern rosebushes in the garden we share, neither of us could stand the sight of another pair of pruners or loppers. "Well, the Hybrids might be pruned," Bob pointed out, "but you haven't touched the old garden roses; I haven't looked at the apple trees; and neither of us has even mentioned the wisteria."

"Let's skip them," I suggested, "and see what happens when we let them go for a year."

We saw, and it wasn't always a pretty sight.

My rationale for neglecting the heirloom roses stemmed from commercial greed. Although we're in the business of growing garden roses for the sale of their blossoms, we'd never been successful with the old-timers, in part because of their relatively short stems. I figured that we'd leave the gangly bushes alone and harvest the long-stemmed blossoms that developed at their tips, thereby pruning later. Boy, was I kidding myself.

The unpruned dowagers blossomed, of course, but the stems that held most blooms were too spindly to hold the flowers erect. The lovely glistening white Damask rose 'Madame Hardy' (which is small anyway) would nod on any stem longer than 3 inches. Also, blossoms were noticeably smaller than those of previous years, when bushes had been pruned. 'Fantan Latour', the celebrated Centifolia rose, was a shadow of its previous self and its stems were embarrassingly short.

Worse yet, because the centers of bushes weren't thinned out at pruning time, worthless wood flourished within their interiors, causing foliage to suffer from poor air circulation. By midsummer, my Hybrid Perpetual rose 'Baroness Rothschild' was white as snow with powdery mildew. "Never again," I swore to myself.

Bob's apple trees fared even worse. We were told that last year's apple crop was down anyway, because of an unusually wet spring (fertile pollination is impeded when weather is moist). Our yield wasn't merely down, the apples themselves were diminutive compared to previous years, particularly on varieties such as Winter Banana, Cox's Orange Pippin, and all members of the family whose names end in Delicious. The tiny apples tasted and cooked perfectly well, but weren't appetizing until they were cut up.

Like roses (apples' first cousins), apple trees are so ambitious in spring that they thrust out more growth than they can ultimately support. Spindly laterals can be thinned out, of course, but at pruning time, the majority (all stems growing toward the center of the tree) should be sacrificed with an eye toward next year's crop. Left unpruned, apple trees are expected to support last season's weak wood plus more to come.

Only the wisteria stood up to our lazy ways. Anyone who has ever grown wisteria will vouch that you can practically watch it grow. Properly cultivated plants that are only ten years old look like they're a hundred. Annual pruning of wisterias involves cutting lesser wood off superior wood that's aiming in the direction you intend. Last year, everything was left, lesser or not.

When dense masses of buds began to swell, I regretted putting my pruners away. By the time they blossomed, however, I was no longer sorry. Individual racemes (the drooping wisteria bloom) may have been shorter than those of previous years, but there were lots more of them.

Those same gardeners who testify to wisteria's rambunctious growth will also tell you that you can get by without pruning wisterias only for so long. In fact, I think every other year is a must; otherwise you'll lose control.

We've learned our lesson. Although we might skip the wisteria every other year, we wouldn't dream of leaving heirloom roses or apple trees unpruned again.

Confessions of a Garden Six-Pack Junkie

◌

For the first several years I messed around with horti-culture, I thought that gardeners who planted seeds either had greenhouses or were too cheap to buy seedlings in handy-dandy, pop-out, plastic six-packs. Consequently, during those days, my yard looked like a grown-up version of our neighborhood nursery.

I planted the varieties of flowers and vegetables my grower carried, not necessarily those I wanted. For instance, although I preferred dark-blue lobelia to any other shade, I made do with sky blue when cobalt wasn't available. When pink petunias went out of fashion, I planted red ones like my neighbors.

My vegetable garden was no great shakes either. "Why don't you carry arugula or butter lettuce?" I complained as I fingered the pale romaines.

"Arugula grows too fast to keep in pop-out trays and most people only ask for romaine," my nurseryman assured me, rotating his flats of seedlings.

After a few seasons, when I could no longer bear second or third best among what my garden grew, I reluctantly explored the world of seed. Now I wonder why I waited so long.

Gardening from seed has little to do with economics. Yes, seeds are cheaper than seedlings, but that's irrelevant—the array of choices is the ticket. More than 90 percent of all the flowers and vegetables that you've ever heard of produce seed that some seedsman lists in a mail-order catalog.

Almost as important as getting your hands on special seeds is the joy of starting them early. If you garden where caution warns to postpone sowing seeds until all danger of frost has passed, get a head start on spring by beginning indoors, and you don't need a greenhouse. Although the majority of seeds like to germinate in 70° F. soil, an enormous number (vegetables particularly) would just as soon sprout in a 55° F. environment—not a problem in most households. Even seeds said to germinate only in 90° F. will grow on the sill of a sunny kitchen window.

Always sow seeds in a medium prepared especially for germination, never in garden soil, which has to be baked first and will smell terrible. Although sterile soil seems fancy because it's loaded with expensive-sounding additives like perlite and vermiculite, it's actually cheap. Besides, you don't need much.

You can plant seeds in the same flats the pros use, including the pop-out plastic molds. The seed receptacles I prefer are peat pots—compressed peat pellets with an indentation on top for receiving a seed (or two) and mesh netting around all sides to retain the pot's shape after expanding from water saturation (to ten times their dry size). After placing seeds in the clever depositories, soak them. Then, cover flats of peat pots with a thin layer of sterile soil and soak them again.

As your determination grows for gardening from seed, you'll learn tricks for bettering your odds at germination. Keeping everything moist is no secret, of course, but many people don't realize that numerous seeds benefit from soaking in water for six hours, or overnight, and that others germinate faster if their shells are nicked just before sowing.

I still grow romaine lettuce, although the seeds I plant produce a different variety from the one my nursery still carries—not as consistent in size, but ever so much more flavorful. I also grow vegetables that you'll see neither as seedlings in nurseries or as adults in supermarkets—Borlotto Italian shell beans whose bushes produce pretty rosy-red pods in sixty-eight days; King Midas carrots that bear early and last long, extending their harvest from sweet fingerlings to succulent 9-inch tapers; French Otina leeks that are delicious when eaten raw or sautéed when the size of a pencil; and white Lisbon scallions that produce long white shafts and juicy green tops. Thanks to a whole new world of seed, I grow arugula all year round. My lobelia? They're the darkest blue I've ever seen.

Tricking Hibiscus

M aude knows all about gardening," residents of my small hometown in southwest Louisiana used to say about my paternal grandmother. "She has the prettiest yard in town." My grandmother taught me tricks I've never improved on to this day: how to spot the leader on a sweet pea vine so that others could be cut out early; how to snip magnolia blossoms and float them in bowls of water without ever touching their petals, which brown if fingered; and how to coerce stubborn crape myrtle trees to be columnar rather than squat. While I bless my grandmother for passing on a love for these plants, there's one I wish she hadn't addicted me to—hibiscus, specifically *Hibiscus Rosa-sinensis,* the Chinese or tropical hibiscus. Once you're smitten by these wondrous flowers, you, too, may go to pains to grow them.

I no longer live in the bayous of Louisiana, where the climate obliges hibiscus and other members of the *Malvaceae* family, such as cotton, okra, hollyhock, and swamp mallow. But besides living in the wrong zone for growing them, there are two other reasons why I ought to ignore hibiscus.

First, I'm partial to fragrant flowers and hibiscus doesn't carry a whiff of perfume. Second, blossoms are almost as ephemeral as daylilies. I got over my fragrance fetish where hibiscus are concerned because of the electrifying colors, dazzling texture, and chiseled architecture of their blossoms. I also no longer mind that blooms rarely hold their beauty for more than a day or two because mature plants flower at breakneck speed. So, I grow two hibiscus in large containers and trick them into imagining that they live in a subtropical zone.

My hibiscus are planted in square 18-inch redwood containers fitted with casters so that I can wheel them into sunny deck areas during summer and inside near a warm window for four months of winter. I don't pretend, of course, that my plants perform as well as they would if planted in ground warmed year-round, but they're nothing to sneeze at.

Container culture suits hibiscus well because they demand perfect drainage. In fact, gardeners fortunate enough to grow hibiscus in the earth, dig holes deeper than those required for most plants and put gravel in the bottom to further ensure quick water runoff. In keeping with the advice offered by hibiscus pros, my potting medium is composed equally of garden loam, leaf mold, and sharp sand.

In late autumn, when I'm certain that winter is just around the corner, I push my containerized hibiscus to an area where they can dry out and lighten their load. Then,

I move them to their winter hideout and give them just enough water to keep them alive, without encouraging new growth.

Once all danger of frost is past, I wheel my plants back out to their sunny deck, prune them more severely than is strictly necessary (which I'm convinced ensures exhibition-quality blooms), water them frequently, and begin a well-balanced, bimonthly fertilizer program that I don't let up until the end of August. They bloom their heads off.

Since overwintering plants indoors is such a nuisance (even with casters, containers are cumbersome), I've honed my hibiscus to two varieties. My favorite is White Wings Compacta, a diminutive version of the common White Wings—a five-petaled, white, red-throated beauty with an exaggerated, tobacco-red stigma-bearing style. My second is American Beauty, a luscious pink single with a fat, conspicuous golden-yellow style.

Hibiscus fanciers ask me why I don't grow any of the double, showier varieties. I tell them it's because I prefer simplicity to frills, but I really think it has something to do with Grandmother Maude.

Garden Gadabouts

A lthough it's usually a bad idea to give gardeners a plant you think they should grow, there are exceptions. Some years ago, a friend brought me a potted *Digitalis alba* (white foxglove). "I've put this in a container," she said, "because I wasn't sure you'd want it in the garden—it's a rampant reseeder, you know." My friend went on to explain that until I was certain I liked her gift, I should keep the plant on my sundeck. "Of course, I think it would look smashing in that corner where you seem to fancy white, gray, and silver," she couldn't resist suggesting.

When the foxglove blossomed, I knew I coveted it for keeps, and not just on my sundeck. I transplanted the albino digitalis into the garden, but to show who was boss, not precisely where my friend had suggested. As the creamy-white trumpet-shaped blossoms with maroon-flecked throats matured, I collected their seeds—hundreds of them. From a single spike of blooms, I harvested more seeds than I intended to replant, then left the other stalks alone.

The following spring, I sowed seeds at every spot in the garden that I imagined could benefit from tall white exclamation marks. I needn't have bothered. Mother Nature, with a possible assist from some active birds and prevailing winds, had decided to strew seeds not only over my garden, but throughout my neighbor's as well. By the next year, it looked as though we were growing foxgloves commercially. I've since given digitalis seeds or seedlings to every visitor who so much as hinted at foxglove admiration (warning them, of course, that digitalis blossoms are dangerously toxic).

What amazed me almost as much as its hell-bent determination for survival, was that this digitalis proved color-true from seed—successive plants always bloomed white. That might not seem such a big deal if you don't know that most plants that blossom with white flowers revert to their mother color when they reseed. Buddleia (commonly known as the butterfly bush because of its ability to summon butterflies), for instance, is available in white. Seedlings from white mother plants, however, almost always come up some shade of lavender or purple.

Overworked gardeners bless reseeders such as digitalis. What a comfort it is to admire blossoms one year and know nothing extraordinary must be planned to include them in next year's planting scheme! This praise extends to the herb patch, too, where culinary favorites such as thyme and oregano become pets because they reappear each spring, whereas annuals such as basil are resented for their insistence on flourishing only one year.

Another fine annual that imagines itself a perennial is nicotiana—the quintessential flower for the working person. You never have to fret that nicotiana is smelling up your garden without you there to appreciate it, for nicotiana blossoms don't open until dusk surrounds its trumpet-shaped vanilla-scented flowers. Nicotiana reseeds as though it lives in fear of extinction.

Other favored garden runabouts include verbascum, commonly known as mullein (stay away from *Verbascum olympicum,* which, as its name implies, is an athletic sky-scraper); dianthus (the heirloom varieties are more reliable at self-sowing than their modern hybrid offspring); *Nigella damascena,* better known as love-in-a-mist or devil-in-the-bush, whose blue, white, or rose flowers look almost as enticing as their common names imply; linaria, also known as toadflax (watch out for strains so invasive they become pesty); and some lavender, particularly *Lavandula Stoechas* (Spanish lavender).

Whatever else you do, make certain you admire these garden gadabouts enough to grant them lifelong admittance to your garden, because once you plant them, they're resident tenants.

Anyone need seed from white foxglove?

Seed Shelf Life

$\sim$

One of the recipients of seeds from my *Digitalis alba* (white foxglove) wrote that her seeds never sprouted in spite of the care she gave their planting, which she related precisely. "Where did I go wrong?" she wondered.

That letter haunted me for the next several days because it was clearly written by a devoted gardener who obviously craved white foxglove. I began suspecting that she wasn't the one at fault.

Sure enough, to my horror, I discovered that the foxglove seeds I dispatched weren't entirely fresh—seeds collected during more than one year were stored in jars that looked identical. Although seed containers were labeled by variety, they didn't all record dates. I had obviously sent my reader seeds rendered inviable from careless handling. I immediately dispatched fresh ones.

Although there are stories of seeds from evening primroses lasting fifty years and of certain lotus germinating after a thousand years, most such stories are exaggerated or took place under unusual circumstances. Still, seeds of certain vegetables, such as beets, cucumbers, and radishes, reliably remain viable for up to ten years. Seeds of most annuals and vegetables, however, last only two to three years, and that long only provided they are kept cool and free from moisture.

The rule of thumb for conditions surrounding safe seed storage is that the sum of the temperature (degrees F.) plus the relative humidity should not exceed 100 (actually, humidity is more important than temperature because it allows for the growth of microorganisms that degrade seed quality). Containers for storing seed should be airtight and moistureproof. Canning jars with new lids and glass containers with good rubber seals are ideal, as are baby-food jars.

Seed jars should be kept cool, always out of rays of bright sunlight. Ground-floor closets are good, as are basements and cellars. Seeds of woody herbaceous plants (most perennials) should be stored in the refrigerator.

Seeds of certain plants are so ephemeral that they should never be stored no matter what care you give them. These include asparagus species, perennial delphinium, franklinia, geranium, gerbera daisy, magnolia, and even the ubiquitous *Salvia splendens*.

If you order seeds that are to be shipped wet in moistened sphagnum moss, simultaneously pledge to plant them as soon as you receive them. Seeds of tropical plants such as anthurium, philodendron, ginkgo, and clivia are shipped the minute after they're harvested and must be sown immediately if expected to germinate.

Seeds of the vast majority of annuals, vegetables, and perennials need no special attention at planting time. For those with particularly hard shells or others treated with chemical inhibitors designed to prevent germination, however, two particular steps are called for: scarification and soaking.

The seed coats of some seeds are so hard that they cannot easily absorb moisture and must be scarified in order to become permeable to water. Scarification is nothing more than nicking seeds with a knife, sandpaper, or a file.

Soaking seeds has two purposes. First, like scarification, it softens hard seed coats. Second, soaking leaches out the chemical inhibitors. As a final bonus, soaking seeds shortens the time necessary for germinating notoriously slow starters.

Whatever else you do with stored seeds, be certain to label their containers: what's inside and when they were harvested. If I had followed my own advice, I would have never made that poor reader doubt her horticultural acumen.

Gardening Under Trees

W hen new homeowners plant a garden, they most always begin with trees. Good idea. "We'll just plant a few trees at the corner of the lot," they say. "They'll give the yard backbones, help keep out wind, and we may some-day enjoy their shade."

Although these horticultural newcomers are basically correct, they don't realize that as their inevitable passion for gardening grows, land becomes more and more precious nearer and nearer those trees. "Why didn't someone men-tion that eucalyptus drop everything they grow, including whole limbs?" they whimper.

Before committing to whether or not you intend to plant under your garden's trees, learn first which trees accept neighbors and which never consider it. The broadest rule of thumb is that sun-friendly plants like to grow under deciduous trees but not beneath heavily foliated ever-greens. Deciduous trees drop their foliage during winter, affording plants underneath them extra sunlight when it's most scarce. Also, leaves from deciduous trees are rich sources for nutrients that break down slowly (many native forest plants such as ferns and wild lilies depend on these leafy carpets for survival).

But all deciduous trees are not created equal. Poplar trees, for instance, are lousy choices for most gardens. Although poplars are so voracious you can almost watch them grow, and in spite of the fact that they stubbornly resist wind, they are selfish, demanding as much ground space as their invasive roots can invade and more than their fair share of water. Poplars send out massive runners in a full circle around their trunks. These persistently thirsty rootlets rest just at ground level, poised to slurp up water as soon as it hits the ground. Nearby plants with fibrous root systems haven't a chance.

Deciduous fruit trees, on the other hand, are ideal trees for underplantings, as are hawthorn, liquid ambar, birch, Japanese maple, and dogwood. These trees not only share four months of sun with everything planted nearby (because they're leafless that long), their roots sink deep in the ground. Like poplars, many fruit trees have feeder roots. Unlike poplars, however, these fruit trees concentrate their hairlike roots in a circle 2 feet around their trunks. Anything planted farther away poses no threat for food or water.

Bulbs—whole sheets of them—are one of the most satisfying plantings beneath trees. Crocuses can be planted right up to tree trunks because their corms are planted so shallow. Bulbs that require deep planting, such as daffodils, tulips, and hyacinths, should be placed at least 3 feet away from tree trunks.

Three feet is also the proper planting distance for climbing plants expected to grow into trees. A climber must, of course, be well matched to its host. Apples and roses were meant for each other, probably because they're botanical cousins and require almost identical care.

Unless you want a climber to gobble up its host, never plant anything as voracious as wisteria or house-eating roses near trees. Massive redwood trees often stand up to the weight, as do stately conifers, but small- to midsized trees will eventually topple from such heft.

If you worry that a plant of your choice won't get sufficient water or nutrients under the tree, consider container planting. Confined to containers, scads of annuals, perennials, and small shrubs are delirious when placed under trees, mostly because they appreciate shade from midday sun.

I'm told that certain varieties of common trees such as walnut and pine secrete a substance that retards the growth of anything planted nearby—a devious scheme by Mother Nature for warding off squatters. You might confirm that before planting a walnut or pine, but you can take my word about eucalyptus.

Sudden Shade

Ten years ago, when Bob Galyean and I planted a fragrant garden, sun lovers were featured. Except for the shade cast by a row of native California willows along one side, the garden enjoyed full sun. "In a few years, we can consider rhododendron, hosta, and sweet woodruff," Bob said, "but for now, we don't dare plant anything that can't hold up to this sunlight."

The garden was a marvel, and one plant after another outperformed itself, but none more nobly than chamomile and lemon verbena.

Originally, the chamomile was confined to a knoll bordering a thicket of *Magnolia stellata* (star magnolia). Then, it performed so magnificently that Bob planted an entire lawn from seed. Gardeners who visited from England ate their hearts out over that lawn because of the conditions we so nonchalantly afforded chamomile—lean sandy soil, perfect drainage, and, best of all, full sun (scarce commodities in Britain).

At the edge of the lawn, we planted lemon verbena, specifically *Aloysia triphylla,* which thrust itself 6 feet every season. Plants were not only handsome, their foliage was so redolent that they actually served as a culinary substitute for lemon. To cap off the fragrant affair, we planted a row of hawthorn trees just behind the rosemary. Like the chamomile and rosemary, the hawthorns were in pig heaven.

Two years ago, I started noticing patches of bare ground in the chamomile lawn. It was also then that I first complained that the lemon verbena was looking particularly lanky. I accused Bob of extending his fertilizer program to the herbs (most prefer hunger), but he assured me he hadn't. Even though it glared before me in the full light of day, it never dawned on me what had happened.

Then, family members visited and we dragged out photo albums of the garden from its inception. When I saw a photograph of the puny bareroot hawthorn trees we planted, I realized the problem at once—shade. Those hawthorn saplings were now near maturity and shading everything planted underneath the reaches of their outstretched limbs.

The same conditions existed elsewhere in the garden—Lombardy poplars that were 6 feet tall when planted bareroot were now over 40 feet and reaching; a scrawny pair of persimmon saplings grew into billowing plump trees massed with large foliage; and a hedge of *Viburnum Tinus,* which takes a decade to mature, finally had. Birch trees planted from no larger than 15-gallon containers stood like towering shrouds over slender pittosporum bushes that once grew fat.

Even the yews, which are painstakingly slow growing, were beginning to deprive nearby daphne bushes of a full day's sun. It was time to rethink the garden, sunwise. Although available sunlight was still there for the taking, the tallest plants were taking it.

Suddenly, flowers, herbs, and ground covers previously taboo in our sun patch were viable possibilities. We planted rhododendron that appreciate dappled shade where they would have fried ten years earlier. Sweet woodruff that shrivels from the sun like a vampire now carpets an area cast in shade from honeysuckle that had finally climbed up a massive tripod camouflaging a telephone pole. Foxglove reached 6-foot heights because of cool shade from a nearby magnolia that quite outdid itself.

We don't regret planting any of the sun lovers that now rob the garden of half its available sunlight—those poplars provide a welcome windbreak, the fruits of the persimmons afford the garden color in an otherwise bleak season, and the hawthorns not only produce blossoms with a balsamic fragrance in spring, they sport colorful haws (hawthorn's fruit) in fall.

At the same time you decide on vertical plants for your garden, start reading up on shade. Eventually, you may be forced to garden in it.

Seed Gardening in the Shade

ↂ

Since roses are my long suit, until two years ago, I'd always been a sun worshiper. I'd developed such tunnel vision for plants that like full-day sun, I never even considered gardening in the shade. Then, I ran out of sunny space, and turned to a gardening guru for advice. "I've got a commodious shady area on the fringe of a field of roses that's cast in dappled shade by native willows," I told him. I can start seeds of whatever you suggest now and set them out later, but aren't shade plants fussy?"

"Not nearly so fussy as those roses of yours," he snapped back, then went on to explain that if I waited until the soil warmed slightly, I could skip the bother of starting seedlings indoors, planting instead directly where I wanted plants to grow. "Tell you what," my guru suggested, "take that shady area off your list of places to worry about, and just leave it to me. In a week or two, I'll send you seeds of what I think should grow there."

I do as told in situations like these. In ten days, a rattling envelope arrived with a note of instructions. "Your seed-starter set has three surefire winners," my mentor began. "The foxglove is *Digitalis alba* (as pure white as foxglove gets), the myosotis (forget-me-not) is a strain of *Myosotis scorpioides* (lavender blue with a white eye), and the impatiens is *Impatiens Balfourii,* commonly called poor man's orchid because its free-blooming, two-tone mauve flowers vaguely resemble orchids. Create your own design under those willows, but keep in mind that the foxglove may reach 6 feet, the impatiens will top off at 3, and the forget-me-nots won't grow taller than 10 inches."

Although my overall goal was a natural look, I let height dictate the free-form undulating planting scheme—mostly foxglove at the rear of the beds, mainly forget-me-nots in the front, and impatiens in between. I remembered, however, how easily such planting schemes look regimented. To prevent that, I sowed occasional foxglove seeds toward the front of each bed and interspersed the other two annuals so that they never formed straight lines.

The results were spectacular. Visitors swore they never saw foxglove so tall, impatiens more floriferous, or forget-me-nots so comely. At the end of an extended blooming season (April to November), I decided that shade gardening from seed was for me, but not to mess with success.

Within two days of the anniversary of its planting, I marched back to the site of my triumph with fresh seeds in hand. I needn't have bothered; Mother Nature had the same scheme in mind, with hundreds of seedlings well on their way to maturity. I ended up thinning out two thirds of them so that those I left might coexist.

For faulty reasons best known to me before this delightful experience occurred, I had always considered shade a liability to the garden. Worse yet, I equated shade with snails. That was foolish. Not only was my trilogy of annuals relatively impervious to munching insects, they were disease resistant, too.

Now, of course, I'm on a constant search for unclaimed shady areas, reveling in my days out of the sun. This year, for instance, my seed order listed four varieties of violas to sow under a grove of deciduous magnolias and two species nicotiana for carpeting beneath a birch grove.

As my quest for shade lovers continues, I'm bound to meet annuals that must be replanted each year (the way basil behaves in the herb garden). Until I do, I'm tickled pink with the reseeders.

Dear Garden Diary

Purple hyacinths begin to bloom" were the first five words Thomas Jefferson entered in the garden diary he began on Monticello, March 30, 1766. As his passion for horticulture grew, Jefferson filled volumes of separate diaries devoted to farm and garden. In time, he also became botanically precise and dutifully recorded names of new plants in proper horticultural lingo along with elaborate plans for installing them. Whether in a proper notebook, computer memory, or jotted on a wall calendar, diaries are essential to good gardening; they're also as personal as love letters because no other garden, not even the one next door, has a timetable identical to yours.

My garden, for instance, is protected from prevailing westerly winds by a row of native willow trees planted along the garden's western edge. My neighbor's garden offers no such protection, and, although we grow many of the same plants, mine (especially spring bulbs) bloom at least two weeks earlier than his (not because of protection from the wind, but rather because those willows retain heat and boost the soil's warmth).

Conversely, my naked-ladies (the common name of *Amaryllis Belladonna*) bloom two to three weeks later than those in town because we don't have as many concrete surfaces in the country (concrete holds heat well). Similarly, the acacias, flowering fruit trees, and species roses in town begin blossoming much sooner than mine.

Separate varieties of the same flower have their own schedule, too. 'Granada', for instance is always the first of my modern roses to bloom. Similarly, 'Gold Medal' is the last to give up the ghost. In between, I'd be lost without a diary. Sure, I can remember that 'Iceberg' is on the late side, but without a diary, I couldn't tell you if it's before or after my other pet white roses—'Pascali', 'Sheer Bliss', 'Honor', and 'Peaudouce'.

Recording sequence of bloom isn't the only good reason for keeping a diary; planning color schemes is equally important. If your diary reminds you that for the bulk of last February, your garden looked like it belonged to a someone obsessed with yellow, don't plant a lot of late-blooming pink camellias. On the other hand, if your reddish-mauve *Erysimum* 'Bowle's Mauve' blossoms strongly in April, you may want to consider planting purplish-red ranunculus nearby; they make smashing companions and, in most gardens, bloom at the same time. When such happy pairings come along, make note of them. If you imagine that your memory will serve you well as to whether or not there were also competing colors nearby, you're wrong.

Memory should also never be trusted where chemicals are concerned either. If you find that, as much as you detest using it, only the spray of a mild insecticide will erase spring's aphid infestation, write down both the date you sprayed and the strength of the solution used. First, aphids visit certain gardens at the same time (within a two-week period, at least) each year. Second, labels on chemical products have a way of fading or washing off over time, and you never want to use chemicals stronger than the job calls for.

Diaries are also extremely useful for reminding you of improvements your garden could use. If, for instance, you notice in spring that the ornamental pear tree you planted three years ago is already too large for its allocated space, make a note in your diary to move it next January, while it's dormant.

Besides taking good notes, it's also imperative to review them occasionally. I could have saved myself the ravages of a mighty thrip infestation this past May if I had reread last year's diary carefully and armed my roses accordingly.

PART 3

Dining on
the Garden

Kitchen Gardening
in a Pot

A fter living in a city for more than twenty years, my friend Kenner finally had yard space all his own. "My new place came with a garden," he said with enthusiasm. "Actually, the garden proper is shade city—perfect for rhododendron, azalea, and maybe some digitalis," Kenner proclaimed. "But, there's a sunny deck just off the kitchen with plenty of space for pots. Which herbs grow well in containers?"

Kenner's question struck pay dirt. Except for those herbs that grow intolerably large, such as angelica, borage, and dill, most herbs take beautifully to container culture.

Before buying any container in which you intend to cultivate herbs, first make certain that it has ample drainage holes. Herbs aren't particular about the pots or boxes they grow in, but they like dry feet and appreciate quick, thorough drainage. Herbs aren't fussy about the soil they grow in either. In fact, most herbs prefer poor sandy soil to rich garden loam. Although potting mediums sold as all-purpose mix will suffice, if you want to keep herbs hungry (which many gardeners claim intensifies their flavors), add sharp sand to whatever potting soil you have on hand, thereby improving drainage.

Herbs appreciate as much sun as possible and no more water than strictly necessary. Once established in the garden, many herbs, except those in the desert, require no water at all, even during summer. Fertilizers aren't necessary either; in fact, excess fertilizer, like excess water, produces rank woody growth.

If you're a newcomer to growing your kitchen's own herbs, consider beginning with those that most cooks consider the big three: rosemary, thyme, and parsley.

One species of rosemary the herb—*officinalis*—has several forms, including some that blossom with pink, white, or lavender flowers. The finest form is the one seen most often, Tuscan Blue, which is rigidly upright and blossoms with porcelain-blue dainty flowers. All varieties have pungently fragrant, narrow, midgreen to dark-green leaves that are silvery gray underneath.

Rosemary is virtually disease free, and snails and slugs are the only pests that dare attack it. True to its Mediterranean heritage, rosemary flourishes in poor dry soil. Fortunately, rosemary also responds nicely to clipping—just as well, since cooks can't keep their scissors away.

Choosing among varieties of thyme isn't nearly so simple as with other herbs; there are more than four hundred distinct species divided into two groups—those that grow upright and those that prefer a prostrate position. If you're choosing thyme for the kitchen, base your choice on smell. Varieties of thyme are fruit scented: from pineapple to tangy lemon. If you're unsure, settle for *Thymus vulgaris*—the good old English standby.

The parsley most favored by cooks is *Petroselinum hortense,* commonly called Italian flat-leaf parsley. If your patience makes Job seem rash you can start parsley from seeds, but be forewarned that they take an eternity to germinate. Established plants in pop-out plastic containers are readily available, even in supermarkets.

My friend didn't settle only on the obvious. With the help of a terra-cotta pot designed to grow strawberries, Kenner also grows basil (both green and opal, plus another that smells exactly like cinnamon), oregano (varieties that blossom with white flowers are thought to be tastiest), sage (the common variety, *Salvia officinalis,* rather than those known for their ornamental value), and cascading rosemary.

"When I was growing up," Kenner confesses, "I always wondered why my grandmother's cooking tasted so much better than anyone else's. The reason, of course, was that she kept a garden with a ready supply of fresh herbs. Thanks to the pots on my sundeck, now I do, too."

Salubrious Salvia

An ancient Latin proverb goes: *Cur moriatur homo cui salvia crescit in horto?* (Why should a man die when sage flourishes in his garden?). The Latin word derives from a once-held belief that the herb could prolong life. In fact, sage was so exalted for anything that ails you, it was the panacea of herbal medicine in the Middle Ages. As herbs became less prevalent for medicinal purposes, sage stuck around because of its culinary value.

I grow several sages, not because I believe they'll keep me kicking, but rather for their fine taste or visual beauty. Before you, too, commit to any of the more than seven hundred species of *Salvia,* why not taste some?

As far as I and some fine chefs I know are concerned, only one sage should enter the kitchen—*Salvia officinalis,* a shrubby perennial that reaches 18 inches to 2 feet. Stems are square and covered in down; leaves are puckered, gray-green, and shaped like fat blades. Small, purple-blue blooms hover in whorls above leaf axils after plants are two years old. Like all sages, *S. officinalis* likes to grow in nutritious, well-drained soil in full sun. Plants are shallow rooted and should be kept well mulched if taste is the target.

Although they're shorter and not as hardy in winter, there are forms of S. *officinalis* that taste just as good as, and are prettier than, the true species, including Icterina, which has variegated golden leaves, and Purpurascens, which has purple leaves on red stems. Before you imagine how fanciful these colors might appear on a plate of prepared food, however, you should know that all salvias turn green when cooked.

In order to keep plants as shapely as possible, be sure to snip whole sprigs, not just leaves, when harvesting sage. If you've never used fresh culinary sage in your kitchen, you'll be surprised how much nicer it is than dried. It has lots of uses besides the traditional recipes for stuffing, but even fresh it has a pervasive flavor that you don't want to overdo. Try adding just a bit before putting in all you've chopped up, because you can't take it out once it has settled in.

Once certain that you have enough sage to eat, you can have a heyday choosing ornamental varieties of salvia, which bloom in all colors, from pure white to lapis blue and bloodred.

Strictly from misuse, S. *splendens* is the most famous sage in America. Although it's an annual, S. *splendens* grows vigorously to 3-foot heights each season. Even more assertively, it flowers with screaming red blossoms whose color fights with almost everything nearby, especially marigolds and zinnias—the favored companions for spelling out Welcome in municipal plantings.

Far more companionable are varieties such as *S. uliginosa*, whose towering racemes of delicate flowers are true blue; *S. leucantha*, commonly known as Mexican bush sage, whose year-end blossoms look like dusty-rose chenille; *S. Clevelandii*, a native to the chaparral slopes of San Diego County, whose gray-green leaves and tiny blue flowers are both pungently perfumed; and *S. viridis*, whose flowers are insignificant but whose veined leaflike bracts grow beneath them in shades of blue, pink, or white.

Once you settle on the color of an ornamental sage, take cuttings directly from a plant whose precise shade suits you. Salvias are a highly variable family whose seeds often don't bloom true to parentage.

According to hard-core salvia aficionados, no single sage plant should remain in your garden for longer than four years. After that time, maybe even sooner, stems become woody and tough. Cooks, of course, will keep that from happening to their patch of culinary sage.

So Many Cooks, So Much Thyme

If you told gardeners the world over that they could grow but a single herb and cooks that they could season their cuisine with only one herb, they would both overwhelmingly choose thyme. Why shouldn't they? By naming thyme, gardeners "restrict" themselves to more than four hundred species—everything from varieties that creep along the ground to those that grow into perky, upright plants the size of small shrubs. Cooks who choose thyme have singled out an herb that harbors flavors ranging from caraway to lemon.

Since well before Christ set foot on earth, thyme has been praised for its association with, and contribution to, honey. The poet Virgil, who was also a beekeeper, said that thyme "yields the most and best honey." From the earliest records of gardening in the Mediterranean, we know that thyme (already proven irresistible to bees) was widely planted in orchards to ensure that the fruit trees would be pollinated. In early Greece, one of the nicest compliments a man could tell a woman was that she smelled sweet as thyme (as well she might, since women then wore oil of thyme as a perfume). Sheep were put to graze in fields where wild thyme grew because it was said to sweeten their meat.

Species of thyme are divided into two groups: those that grow upright and those that prefer a prostrate position. Both are useful all around the garden and all over the kitchen.

Thymus vulgaris, whether it be the English, French, or German variety, is the perennial thyme most used by both gardeners and cooks. *T. vulgaris* grows to 9 inches in height and is covered in masses of pungent, narrow or broad leaves that may be variegated or grayish green. Most varieties have either soft pink or violet flowers and thin stems.

As you might guess. *T.* x *citriodorus* smells like lemons; what's more, smells strongly of them. Leaves of lemon thyme are small, blooms are pale purple, and there are forms with silver or gold foliage.

T. praecox subsp. *articus,* also known as *T. Serpyllum,* is a creeping ground cover with a form that is generally mat, but with branches that grow up to 6 inches tall. Although it can't be tromped on, creeping thyme accepts light pedestrian traffic (for example, when planted between stones in a garden path), and it freely releases its pungent scent whenever its leaves are bruised. Flowers of most forms are rosy purple, but at least one is pure white, and another has hairy, silvery leaves.

When you visit a nursery that specializes in herbs, you'll be bowled over by the number of different varieties of thyme. What you've just read here barely scratches the surface. There is *T. pseudolanuginosus,* the wooly leaved groundcover; *T. vulgaris* 'Argenteus', the official silver thyme, and hundreds more. Some forms are thought to smell of pine, oranges, or pineapple; others reek of turpentine.

Fortunately, you don't have to grow thyme from seeds and wonder what it will smell like. Buy seedlings instead and sniff for yourself. Only the most diligent gardeners care to cope with thyme's tiny seeds (more than 170,000 per ounce!). Once you establish thyme, new plants can easily be rooted as cuttings in early summer (also ensuring the precise scent or flavor you seek).

Thyme is the quintessential herb for drying; its scent is basic to many blends of potpourri and few herbs rival its ability to harbor special culinary flavors, even when thoroughly dried. If you're going to harvest thyme for drying, do so before the plants bloom. The scent and flavor of flowers pale in comparison to those in leaves, but more important, blossoms fade to unappealing colors.

A Dilly of an Herb

Proper horticultural lingo for a favorite garden herb is *Anethum graveolens,* more commonly known as dill—a derivative of the Saxon word *dilla,* to lull. Mothers used to rub their breasts with dillseed water before nursing their babies, after which infants were said to drop quickly off to sleep. Tranquillity was so closely associated with the herb that dill was lavishly planted in cottage gardens as an antidote to witchcraft. Dill seeds freely release their essential oils when infused in hot water, the liquid from which was used as "gripe water" to ease flatulence in children and to quicken sleep at bedtime.

Dill so closely resembles fennel, to which it is related, that as the famous seventeenth-century herbalist Culpeper said, the likeness "deceiveth many." Both have finely cut foliage and make tall, willowy plants. There a couple of distinct differences though that will allow you to tell one from the other. Dill's foliage is as blue as it is green, and its stems are hollow, whereas fennel's are filled. Dill almost always grows but a single, thick, round stem, fennel branches several skinnier ones.

Because seedlings are difficult to transplant, sow dill seeds where you want them to grow. Although they may take two weeks to germinate, your success rate may be 100 percent. Unlike many herbs that prefer poor soil and minimum irrigation, dill appreciates a moderately rich, moist home, especially when plants are young. Dill tolerates partial shade, but prefers full sun.

For some reason, dill is far more popular in Europe than in America. You never see a boiled new potato in Germany without a dill garnish. Scandinavians treasure dill for what it does for fish, especially salmon. The French use it even in baking cakes and pastries.

Dill's delicate foliage, which branches freely from its main stem, is tasty only when young, before the plant starts to concentrate its energies on producing seed heads. As summer heat increases, leaves start to yellow and wither as the plant diverts energy to flat heads of pale-yellow flowers atop 2- to 3-foot plants. As flowers fade and drop, small, bitter oval seeds form in their places. It's these seed heads that picklers are after. A good trick to collecting seed is to harvest entire flower heads as they begin to ripen (but not spill) and put them in paper bags.

To satisfy all gourmets who frequent your herb patch, plan successive dill plantings from April through July. Leaves of eight-week-old plants can be harvested for pungent additions to an array of recipes. Sow in May those plants you intend to let go to seed. They'll do it just as cucumbers crop.

People have pickled cucumbers with dill for centuries without altering the procedure much. A recipe from 1640 reads as follows: "Gather the tops of the ripest Dill and cover the bottom of the vessel, and lay a layer of Cucumbers and another of Dill till you have filled the vessel within a handful of the top. Then take as much water as you think will fill the vessel and mix it with salt and a quarter pound of allum to a gallon of water and poure it on them and press it down with a stone on them and keep them covered close."

Making dill vinegar is much easier. Simply soak leaves for a few days in a salad vinegar of good quality, or insert a feathery dill stem in a bottle of plain vinegar and leave it there until it begins to yellow. Then remove it, leaving its flavor behind.

Dill is prolific and reseeds freely. If you carefully choose the spot where you grow it, you may never have to replant.

Parsley Up to Par

It's no wonder that parsley is so steeped in history, considering how long it has been treasured. Gardeners wouldn't dream of being without a neat, bright, midgreen edging of parsley around their herb patches, cooks won't lift a spoon in kitchens without it, and herbalists consider parsley vital to most brews.

Although parsley is said to be native to Turkey, the Greeks were the ones to write most about parsley because they believed it to be the herb of Hercules. Fresh parsley was woven into wreaths to crown the heads of victors at athletic games.

Because parsley seeds are so slow to germinate (they are said to visit and return from the devil seven times before they sprout), all sorts of myths were associated with planting parsley. At one time, it was thought that a crop of parsley would flourish only if it was planted either on Good Friday or by a pregnant woman. Today any of us can grow parsley successfully as long as we plant it in early spring in sunny humus-rich soil and give it a fair share of water all summer.

The list of the medicinal values associated with parsley is long: it was once thought to ease the pains of afterbirth and arthritis; to lift the dropsies; prevent halitosis; and to effectively combat coughs, insect bites, and hair vermin. Gastronomically, parsley is thought to be an effective antidote to garlic. Above all else, however, parsley is praised as a diuretic—to "cause urine." In fact, a literal translation of the Greek word for parsley is "stone breaker." Today's herbalists still value parsley as a rich source of calcium, riboflavin, thiamin, and vitamins A, C (more concentrated than in oranges), and E.

Even though it's usually grown as an annual, parsley is actually a biennial. In temperate climates where it doesn't freeze, parsley stops growing during the winter, but leaves one foot of roots in the ground. Early spring triggers the formation of a stalk that develops greenish-yellow flowers, then grayish-brown seeds. Cooks who are also gardeners treat parsley as an annual because they're interested only in its leaves, and want them to be fresh. Although I find dried parsley thoroughly dull, I believe frozen chopped parsley is an acceptable substitute for the real stuff. If you've never tried it, keep a jar of chopped parsley in the freezer and use its contents as needed during dreary-gardening months.

Because parsley is so slow to germinate, weed well the areas where you intend to sow seeds and hope that your tiny parsley seeds sprout before the weeds do (count on a good three weeks, whether or not you're pregnant). To facilitate even broadcasts, before sowing parsley's superfine seeds, mix them with sharp sand. To keep plants well fed, apply fertilizers high in nitrogen (parsley seems especially fond of fish emulsion) in early spring and immediately following major harvests.

Although it's the quintessential herb for a knot garden, parsley is a favorite in the garden at large, too. To avid gardeners, the fact that parsley's finely fringed foliage is also useful in the kitchen is pure lagniappe.

It's difficult to pinpoint parsley's fragrance. Mostly, fresh parsley smells like just that, fresh. It also has a wholesome, uplifting zip to it, as though you can actually sniff all those nutrients.

By far, the favorite variety among Europeans is *Petroselinum hortense,* commonly called Italian single-leaf parsley (there is also a spiffy heirloom variety known as Gigante d'Italia, which bears large sprays of flat, shiny, full-flavored, dark-green leaves). For some reason, *P. crispum,* the variety with curly leaves, has caught on stronger in the United States (at least at the supermarkets). I grow both, preferring to eat the European varieties and look at the curly ones.

Please Eat the Begonias

I'm pleased that edible flowers aren't the rage they were a few years ago; dining tables were beginning to look like grazing fields. Overcome by brightly colored flowers someone proclaimed edible, hostesses got carried away. Once, for instance, I attended a cocktail party where the only hors d'oeuvre served was a dip made from crème fraîche, watercress, and a hint of curry. Begonia blossoms were the only means for getting this ambrosia to your lips.

"I didn't know begonias were edible," I confessed.

"Oh, they're delicious," my hostess assured me, "rather like young crunchy rhubarb."

They weren't bad; neither were they exactly delicious, although they certainly were crunchy. The turgid begonia petals didn't remind me of rhubarb either, but I couldn't declare exactly what they did remind me of, other than something vaguely vanilla. Nevertheless, as the evening progressed, I ate at least two plants.

Although I've never once craved for begonias since that party, I eat other flowers on a regular basis. Nasturtium, for instance. Nasturtiums are surely the most edible plants in the entire world of flora, because all parts of the plant are tasty. Blossoms aren't just pretty in salads, they're agreeably peppery, too. Nasturtium seeds are fine for pickling, and young leaves taste something like watercress, but with a slight honey aftertaste—delicious between slices of sweet-buttered bread.

I don't think any more highly of the taste of rose petals than I do of begonias. Rose hips, however, are another matter, and a zippy ingredient for well-flavored jelly or conserve. Best of all, rose hips are packed with vitamin C.

Although all members of the squash family, even pump-kins, flower with blossoms you can safely eat, none is tastier than zucchini. Picked before their pale-yellow color begins to fade (then stuffed with ricotta cheese, slivered pine nuts, and minced parsley), squash blossoms are delicious when deep-fried. Before getting greedy, however, remember that stems whose young blossoms have been plucked won't bear gourds.

Flowers of herbs taste the way their leaves do, only milder. The blooms of basil, for instance, harbor the identical pungency found in basil's leaves and lend a fanciful touch to a plate of pasta with pesto. Similarly, chopped or whole, flowers of fennel, oregano, sage, and thyme make handsome and flavorful garnishes.

Some herbs are actually more famous for their blooms than for their foliage. Borage flowers, for instance, have always been more precious than the leaves, which have never been better than a poor man's spinach. Once the hairy sepals are pulled off, petals of borage blossoms taste exactly like sweet young cucumbers.

I've never understood the hoopla over culinary uses for *Calendula officinalis,* better known as pot marigold. During the Renaissance, calendulas were prescribed for maladies ranging from toothaches to piles. To me, petals of calendula taste pasty at first, then salty, then medicinal.

Bee balm, on the other hand, flowers with some of the tastiest blossoms that ever flavored a bergamot tea. The Shakers, prominent American herbalists, concocted foliar infusions of bee balm to soothe sore throats, but they saved the blossoms to lend a lemony-mint flavor to fruit cups and jellies.

Don't even wonder about the taste of anemone, autumn crocus, azalea, buttercup, caladium, clematis, datura, delphinium, foxglove, hydrangea, lantana, lily of the valley, lupine, oleander, rhododendron, star-of-Bethlehem, even sweet pea. Not all varieties of these common garden flowers will kill you (unless eaten in large quantities), but they'll either make you sick or give you a splitting headache.

Taste any edible flower you like, although I'll bet you'll never crave a whole bowl of them for dinner. But I have to admit, begonia petals can be downright tasty, especially when they cradle a dollop of flavored crème fraîche.

PART 4

Her Majesty, the Rose

The War of the Roses

⟨∞⟩

As a rosarian, it pains me to admit that my fellow rose buddies are split into two equally ornery camps that rarely see eye to eye—those devoted to heirloom garden roses and others who prefer modern hybrids.

What separates old from new roses? A year—1867, when the French breeders Guillot Fils hybridized 'La France', the first Hybrid Tea rose. Nineteenth-century hybridizers craved roses with high pointed centers, and 'La France' was precisely what they had in mind.

By the beginning of the twentieth century, there were enough new roses around so that names were needed to separate old from new. Those who preferred the older kind began calling them "garden" roses, labeling their offspring "modern." Soon after, the rose world split asunder.

Garden rose aficionados point out that, although their pets usually bloom only once each year (for up to six weeks), they make up for the restricted season with bountiful blossoms. "Also," these diehards incessantly point out, "garden roses are vastly more fragrant than modern hybrids." I suppose if you bothered to sniff every antique garden rose known to man, then every modern variety, you'd find a higher percentage of perfume in heritage roses. That is not to say, however, that modern roses aren't scented.

Someone said that God made Tina Turner to show other women how to walk in high heels. Similarly, I believe God (and Germany's hybridizer Tantau) created 'Fragrant Cloud' in 1963 to put an end to bellyachers who lamented the loss of fragrance in modern roses. The delicious scent of 'Fragrant Cloud' is enough to satisfy the piggiest of perfume fanciers.

"Modern roses are too prissy," garden rose enthusiasts protest, "a little too perfect. We want decadence, not symmetry." Hybrid rose fanciers suggest these complainers wait awhile, that the most perfectly formed of hybrid buds will eventually mature into a buxom irresistibly informal bloom.

Disease resistance is a close call. True, many heirloom varieties are tough old birds, but others such as the famous Hybrid Perpetual 'Baroness Rothschild' are so susceptible to powdery mildew that each August my bushes look as though I shook sacks of flour over their heads. Oddly enough, the modern bushes most adamantly resistant to disease are the one hottest off the hybridizing bench. Landscape roses (as they're getting to be known) such as 'Bonica', 'Carefree Wonder', and 'All That Jazz' demand no spraying and little pruning.

After listening carefully to arguments from both factions of this tempest-in-a-teapot war, I've decided not to surrender to either side but to fight for both.

I wouldn't consider handing over my bushes of the ravishing pure white Damask rose 'Madam Hardy' any more than I'd give up my soft-pink, sumptuously perfumed Centifolia rose 'Fantin Latour', even though both of these beauties blossom only once each year and finish by June.

Neither, however, will I be denied roses from July through October; hence my affection for modern hybrids that blossom satisfactorily every six to eight weeks, over six months of continuous bloom.

I've seen people swoon over roses that made me want to avert my eyes. Similarly, I've noticed eyeballs roll heavenward when I carry on over a bloom of the deliciously fragrant, oversized, clear-pink Hybrid Tea 'Bewitched'; the elegant apricot-blend modern Floribunda 'Sea Pearl'; the madly striped voracious Hybrid Perpetual 'Ferdinand Pichard'; the wickedly alluring young hybrid 'Sexy Rexy'; or any other of my favorites from the rose garden.

When it comes to roses, just as with food, decor, clothing, movies, or anything else, it's all a matter of taste. Still, I'll never forgive Gertrude Stein for that damnable phrase, "A rose is a rose is a rose."

Gertrude was dead wrong.

How Maria Callas
Helped Me
Learn About Roses

∞

A lthough there is considerable controversy surrounding the precise development of the genus *Rosa,* its general evolution is well documented. First, there were wild species roses. Then the Renaissance came along and hybrids emerged. Next, free-flowering varieties from the Orient reached Europe, and eventually nineteenth-century breeders developed the modern rose. If you grasp this four-step evolution, the rest is easy—roses that no one is certain where to rightfully place in history fall into order.

I never had a problem identifying species roses; they blossom only once each year and usually have gargantuan growth habits. Nor have I ever had difficulty spotting a rose hybridized after 1867—the year of the first Hybrid Tea rose's debut. Modern roses bloom repeatedly, usually on plants known as bushes, as opposed to shrubs.

Still, I had a devil of a time remembering the differences among all ten rose families between species and modern roses—Gallica, Damask, Alba, Centifolia, Moss, China, Portland, Bourbon, Hybrid Perpetual, and Tea.

The Moss roses were easy to identify because mossing appears on more than buds and the prickly adornments are almost always apparent whether or not there are also blooms. The Chinas were easily identified, too. First, their blossoms are whimsically formed, almost as if by accident, and the growth of the bushes is airy (plenty of space between branches).

I often guessed correctly that an unidentified rose was a Bourbon because blossoms belonging to this family are notoriously perfumed. Similarly, I learned that Tea roses are easy to spot because of the symmetry of their blossoms. Most Gallicas bloom in strong colors, often in stripes. The majority of Damask roses are pink and powerfully fragrant, and grow on bushes with gray-green, elongated downy foliage. Albas are predominantly white or near white and blossom on lofty bushes (often over 6 feet). Centifolias produce heavily petaled blossoms but on lanky bushes. The blossoms of Portland roses are well shaped but short stemmed. Hybrid Perpetual roses—unlike most heirloom rose groups—repeat their blossoms during summer (although with nowhere the regularity of modern hybrids).

After growing hundreds of varieties of members of these ten families and learning to identify most of them on sight (without benefit of a plant identification tag), I still couldn't remember their respective ages. "Tell me," a visitor would ask, "did this Moss rose here come before or after that Centifolia over there?" My mind would agonizingly grind out the progression of families. "I've got to make this easier to remember," I swore to myself, "this delayed expertise is embarrassing."

I recalled that when I was a boy my favorite science teacher had told me about "ROYGBIV," the key word for remembering the colors of the rainbow in order. I realized, however, that I'd never wrap my tongue around a word like "GDACMCPBHPT," the first letters to the ten families between species and modern roses. How to string together Gallica, Damask, Alba, Centifolia, Moss, China, Portland, Bourbon, Hybrid Perpetual, and Tea?

One day while strolling past a border of my favorite old roses, I listened to a recording of Maria Callas singing *Norma*. "Why not map this road with a tribute to your favorite diva?" I thought.

"*G*enuine *D*evotees *A*lways *C*heer *M*aria; *C*hildish *P*eople *B*less *H*igh-*P*itched *T*enors"—the words tumbled out of my mouth. I realized it was corny, of course, and didn't tell anyone about it at first. I've attempted time and again to improve on my silly phrase, but I keep returning to it.

Make up your own mnemonic saying, but whatever else you do, get to know these beauties that led to the modern rose—they pave a handsome road.

The Madame and Her
Clutch of Noisettes

I n determination to grasp the evolution of roses from Gallicas (the oldest recognized distinct family of roses) to the modern Hybrid Tea, most gardeners don't have time to consider offbeat clans. That's a pity, because some of the most wondrous roses ever known are only distantly related to recognized first families. Noisettes, for instance.

John Champney, an early-nineteenth-century rice farmer in South Carolina, is considered to be the father of Noisette roses. Whether or not Champney himself mixed the pollen (many rose historians claim that zealous bees were responsible), it seems certain that 'Champney's Pink Cluster' came to be when pollen from a gadabout stud rose from China was scrambled with that from an unidentified musk rose. The affair resulted in a climbing rose that flowered throughout summer.

Philippe Noisette, an ambitious young nurseryman in nearby Charleston, so admired Champney's find that he asked for hips and harvested their seeds. Noisette struck pay dirt with one of his seedlings—'Blush Noisette', which blossomed like crazy and smelled strongly of cloves.

Momentum for the family's development gained impetus when Philippe sent seeds to his Parisian brother, Louis. Not only did Louis recognize immediately the potential of these new roses, he also knew how to improve them by mating them with favored French roses of the time. Louis's scheme worked, for the young American roses fancied their French lovers and notorious children were born.

While some Noisette roses form large graceful shrubs, most are vigorous climbers; all are free-bloomers, whose flower petals are silky and softly colored. Although I've grown numerous Noisette roses and admired even more, 'Madame Alfred Carrière' is my pick of the litter. The Madame is also a splendid choice for silencing the feud between enthusiasts of modern roses and old garden rose fanciers because its blossoms look and smell like old-fashioned roses, but they occur with regularity from late spring into autumn, like those of modern hybrids. Few white climbing roses of any age dare challenge the Madame's overall performance.

Plants of 'Madame Alfred Carrière' grow staunchly upright—easily to the top of an 8-foot pillar in two growing seasons, then over the same distance horizontally if they have support. Foliage is large, midgreen, reasonably disease resistant, and plentiful. Blossoms, which have a charming habit of nodding for good viewing from below, are creamy white tinged slightly with pink, and loosely but lovingly formed. Due to their unmistakable Tea rose ancestry, blooms are exquisitely perfumed.

Although no one threatens the Madame's family preeminence, two vigorous siblings are almost as famous—'Allister Stella Gray' and 'Gloire De Dijon'.

Instead of removing the sturdy trunk of a 3-foot-wide Monterey cypress tree whose top had fallen to a windstorm, I decided to leave 10 feet of it to support 'Allister Stella Gray'. Not only did the ravenous Mr. Gray scramble over the top of the trunk in two years, subsequent seasons brought cascading bowers of bloom 2 feet in all directions. Tight yellow buds form in instant-nosegay clusters, which mature into quartered, tea-scented creamy-white blossoms.

'Gloire De Dijon' is thought to be the result of a cross between an unidentified Tea rose and 'Souvenir de la Malmaison', the famous Bourbon rose. Whatever the parenting, the issue is superb, with yellow-tinted-apricot blossoms that are both large and richly fragrant.

Even though its irresistible blooms are sharply fragrant and lemony yellow, steer clear of Noisettes such as 'Lamarque' if your garden's winter temperatures dip below 20° F. on five consecutive nights. If you have an unclaimed southern wall, however, you'll be hard pressed to find a finer companion for it than a Noisette rose, even a tender one, but especially 'Madame Alfred Carrière'.

Who Hybridized
That Rose?

∞

When I first started growing roses, I couldn't have cared less who hybridized them. Hybridizing seemed like such a crapshoot that the breeders who scrambled rose pollen seemed irrelevant.

"You're much too serious about roses to ignore their makers," a consulting rosarian said to me, then asked me to name my five favorite Hybrid Teas.

" 'Color Magic', 'Pristine', 'Medallion', 'Mr. Lincoln', and 'Bewitched'," I snapped back.

"There you are," he responded, "The first three you mentioned were all hybridized by Bill Warriner for Jackson & Perkins." My guru went on to explain that rose hybridizers keep a look in mind when they create new varieties. "If you also like that look, then you should pay attention to a breeder's whole line."

This quickly proved to be sound advice. When I bought a copy of *Modern Roses* (the bible for rosarians interested in rose lineage), I found that a hybridizer in New Zealand, Sam McGredy, also had a breeding platform that suited me. In 1971, McGredy introduced 'Picasso', a red rose whose petals are randomly splashed with white, no two alike. The look was so distinct that it was described as being "hand-painted." The public's response was so encouraging that McGredy began churning out hand-painted roses with satisfactory regularity, most notably 'Matangi' (vivid orange and silver) in 1974 and 'Sue Lawley' (medium red edged in light pink) in 1980.

Gardeners hooked on fragrance should check out the rose varieties bred by the Tantau family in Germany, especially 'Fragrant Cloud', a lipstick-red buxom rose that many people consider to be the most fragrant rose ever hybridized. Other strongly perfumed varieties from Tantau include the cherry-pink 'Prima Ballerina', the lilac 'Blue Moon', and 'Duke of Windsor', a vermilion rose with a prodigious nose.

Another German hybridizing family, the Kordes clan, has hybridized a line of roses with unusual winterhardiness, including the orange madly blotched 'Voodoo' and 'Colour Wonder', a coral and cream bicolored rose that's virtually impervious to freezing temperatures.

The Meilland family of France never produced a line of roses; they set their sites on winners, not the least of which is 'Peace'—surely the most famous rose ever. After winning first prize with a Hybrid Tea, they went on to create 'Starina', one of the highest-ranked Miniature roses in the world (bright orange and floriferous), as well as a best-selling greenhouse rose, 'Sonia', an appealing combination of apricot and yellow.

The hybridizers mentioned so far barely scratch the surface of the world's makers of heavenly roses. There's Pedro Dot of Spain, who graced the rose world with the creamy-white 'Nevada', one of the loveliest shrub roses ever; Jack Harkness of Yorkshire, England, who recently won an All-America award for 'Amber Queen', an apricot Floribunda that's a blooming fool; and the formidable Ralph Moore (primarily Miniature roses, but dazzling shrubs as well) of Visalia, California.

Besides the pros, several amateur hybridizers are making names for themselves, in the United States and Europe. But the two professional hotshots I believe you should watch are Tom Carruth and Keith Zary. Carruth is research director for Weeks Roses in Upland, California, and Zary maintains the same position with Bear Creek Gardens (the wholesale division of Jackson & Perkins) in Somis, California. Ironically, both hybridizers are making their commercial debut with a Miniature whose name begins with *H*. Carruth's is 'Heartbreaker', a free-blooming pink and white blend. Zary has just introduced 'Hot Tamale', a combination of deep-pink and yellow that's a crowd pleaser.

Next time you spot a rose you really like, don't simply ask its name; find out who hybridized it. You and that breeder may be dreaming of identical roses.

No-Nonsense Roses

L ately, I've been lying to people who ask what is my favorite flower. If I tell them the truth (that I'm incurably rose struck), eight times out of ten, the next words I hear are: "Roses are too much trouble."

I used to argue with these people, assuring them that I could rattle off a litany of relatively carefree varieties of roses. Now I have a two-word answer to the common complaint: "Not Rugosas."

If you're the kind of fair-weather gardener who wants to be outside only when the weather is nice (and would like to have rose blossoms to enjoy indoors when it isn't) but have no intention of pampering, spraying, or pruning rosebushes, please have a look at Rugosas; they're as tough as roses get.

All Rugosa hybrid roses evolved from *Rosa rugosa,* a tough old dowager native to northern China, Korea, and Japan. Drawings of this original Rugosa rose date from A.D. 1000, yet it surely flourished long before. *R. rugosa* has a lot going for it, not the least of which is hardy vigor—a constitution of iron and rambunctious growth to 8-foot heights with equal spread. Large, lightly fragrant, violet-rose flowers blossom throughout summer and are followed (although they often appear concurrently) by plump tomato-shaped hips rich in vitamin C. Finally, the ironclad foliage of *R. rugosa* puts on quite an autumnal show, changing from apple-green to bonfire shades that rival those of maples and liquid ambers.

I don't grow *R. rugosa* for the same reason I don't grow other species roses—it takes up too much space. Hybrids, however, are another matter, and there are some dandy Rugosa hybrids from which to choose; my favorite one blossoms with flowers as pure white as any rose I know.

'Blanc Double De Coubert' was hybridized by the French hybridizing team Cochet-Cochet in 1892. "Blanche," as I call it (because the real name is a tongue-twister), is supposedly the result of a cross between *R. rugosa* 'Repens Alba' (a sport of the already-mentioned species) and the lovely Tea rose 'Sombreuil'. Although not as vigorous as its Rugosa parent, Blanche is plenty spirited—bushes scramble to 5-foot heights with almost as much girth. Foliage is a study in perfection—dark green and so cleverly corrugated with ridges and folds that leaves resemble finely tooled leather. The pristine-white petals that appear to be made of sheer, slightly crinkled tissue paper, surround golden-yellow stamens and emit an intoxicating (practically addicting) fragrance.

Although Blanche is my pet, there are other Rugosa hybrids worthy of consideration. 'Delicata' rarely grows taller then 3 feet but produces bright pink fragrant flowers and orange-red hips. 'Fimbriata' is distinguished by its pale-pink fringed petals. 'F. J. Grootendorst' (and its several forms) is available with crimson, deep-red, clear-pink, or white blossoms. 'Frau Dagmar Hartropp' is a cut-flower favorite because of its enviable habit of churning out fragrant satiny-pink blossoms over a long blooming season. 'Roseraie De L'Hay', named for the sensational garden near Paris, is a liberal producer of intensely fragrant, delicate reddish-purple flowers.

Although I don't give my Rugosa hybrids any special attention when they're planted or spray them during their blooming season, I do prune them. Even then, however, I'm not fussy; I simply decide on a height at which I want them to start growing next season and hack accordingly. Rugosas respond so well to lopping that gardeners are actually encouraged to use hedge clippers to prune them.

On a recent trip to France, I passed miles of Rugosa hybrids planted to separate divided highways—a noble selection for motorway planting and a welcome alternative to oleander.

The Mysterious
Heritage of Hybrid
Musk Roses

⌘

A t the dawn of the twentieth century, a German nurseryman named Peter Lambert planted a seed from (he
claimed) a self-fertilized cross of 'Aglaia', a Rambling rose
originally derived from a cross between *Rosa multiflora* and
'Reve d'Or', a Noisette rose. This seedling, which Lambert
christened 'Trier', demonstrated marked advantages over its
parent, most notably its growth habit, which was shrubby
rather than rambling. As a further bonus, unlike its mother,
'Trier' repeated its bloom cycle. Lambert fancied his 'Trier'
and crossed it extensively, eventually producing a line of
roses he marketed as 'Lambertiana'. Alas, the breed never
caught on with the buying public.

Then the Reverend Joseph Pemberton, a clergyman-
turned-avid-gardener in England's County Essex, tried his
hand at improving 'Trier' by crossing it with various Poly-
anthas, Noisettes, Hybrid Teas, and Tea roses. It is at this
point in the development of the Hybrid Musk roses that
history becomes clouded, for Pemberton seems to have had
an aversion to keeping a stud book for recording precise

parentage. Instead, he preferred (and even instructed his pupils) to develop an eye for the desired qualities for new roses.

To complicate the heritage of the Hybrid Musk roses even further, Pemberton turned over the responsibility for introducing his hybrids to a nurseryman named J. A. Bentall, who not only joined in the hybridizing process himself but also convinced his wife, Anne, to champion the breeding program while he was off fighting in World War I. Although Anne's record keeping was no more diligent than Pemberton's, she obviously had talent, for it was she who bred 'Ballerina' and 'Buff Beauty', two of the world's favorite Hybrid Musk roses.

The name of this family of roses seems destined to stick even though it's a classic horticultural misnomer. Hybrid Musk roses have little to do with the true Musk rose except for their vague lineage via Noisette roses and a fragrance that embraces a musky quality in an otherwise sophisticated bouquet. Although they didn't make much of a splash when their family first appeared, Hybrid Musk roses were "rediscovered" in the 1960s.

The majority of Hybrid Musk roses in commerce today grow into graceful 5- to 6-foot shrubs that bloom profusely in early summer and modestly in autumn. Properly cultivated, Hybrid Musks should be thought of as modern shrub roses and should be planted, fertilized, and pruned with the same careful attention given to recent hybrids.

There are many varieties worthy of attention. 'Autumn Delight', as advertised, is a joy late in the rose season when it freely showers its bushes with sprays of sweetly fragrant flowers that change in color from yellow buds to creamy-white blossoms with red stamens. 'Ballerina' may not be typically Hybrid Musk, but it certainly is a stunner. Individual soft-pink white-eyed flowers are tiny (to 1 inch), but they mass themselves in giant trusses (to 100 blossoms each) and form at the ends of long, graceful stems. 'Buff Beauty' achieved immortality among Hybrid Musk roses primarily because of its color. Although blossoms range in hues from mid-apricot to buff-yellow, they always appear edible, which they are, and smell terrific.

'Kathleen' is a particularly tall lass, quickly scrambling to more than 8 feet. Moderately fragrant blossoms are deep pink, opening to blush pink; almost-single flowers are packed in large clusters. Flowering is followed by the production of showy orange hips. 'Pax' is the most popular Hybrid Musk rose in the United States, chiefly because of its agreeable, tall but graceful growth habits and its sprays of fragrant, semidouble, creamy-white blossoms.

If you've never tried a Hybrid Musk rose in your garden, consider one of the fragrant varieties. You may not smell musk, but you'll like what you smell.

Spotting an
All-America Rose

∞

For years, I was an outspoken critic of certain All-America rose selections. I understood why beauties such as 'Duet', 'Peace', 'Queen Elizabeth', 'Medallion', and a host of other stellar roses carried the prestigious honor, but I cursed those judges who let stinkers like 'Oregold', 'Bing Crosby', 'Love', and 'Sundowner' walk away with the award.

"Why not stop bellyaching and become a judge yourself?" I asked myself. That was three years ago. Now I operate one of twenty-five official All-America Rose Selection test gardens in the United States. I also appreciate that what's All-America in Petaluma, California, may only piddle around in Aimes, Iowa, or fall flat in Wauwatosa, Wisconsin (two other test sites), and vice versa.

All-America Rose Selections, Inc., is a nonprofit research corporation founded in 1938 for the express purpose of evaluating new rose varieties worthy of the All-America stamp of approval. Hybridizers who believe they've come up with potential winners must submit four bushes of each variety to all twenty-five official gardens for a two-year trial.

Officiating judges are instructed to "give roses under test commonsense care," including planting in well-prepared soil, regular spraying, feeding, irrigating, mulching, pruning, and reasonable winter protection.

Currently, four types of rosebushes may be entered for consideration—Hybrid Teas, Floribundas, Grandifloras, Miniatures—as well as the latest group, Landscape roses. Candidates need not originate in the United States if they've never been offered for sale here.

Each entry's performance is scored twice a year, no later than the first of July and again by the first of November. Entries are scored on a 5-point scale (poor to excellent) for fifteen separate attributes, including novelty, form, color, fragrance, vigor, foliage, disease resistance, and repeat bloom. Following each judging session, scores are tabulated and forwarded to the AARS executive director who holds a secret-ballot meeting of the test-garden voting members each January. Winners aren't announced until the following year so that growers have time to bud extra plants of a sure-fire commercial winner.

In order to become the judge of an official garden, you must first operate a demonstration garden for two years, during which time all rules for official gardens apply, including biannual scoring. Although the scores from demonstration-garden judges don't count in final ballots, they're benchmarks for making certain that prospective judges know the difference between great, good, mediocre, and worthless roses.

The first time I judged the entries from my demonstration garden, I agonized for weeks over their final scores. A month later, to my great shock, I learned that the varieties I rated first, second, and third were ranked ninth, fourteenth, and twenty-third by the official judges. I discussed the matter with a judge who's been at the game for years. "Don't worry about it," she said, "just don't let your color biases carry too much weight." I realized that that was just what was wrong. As it happened, the roses leading the trials from that first scoring were shades of vivid orange or red—not my pet colors, especially if no fragrance is attached.

I've since learned to keep my personal opinion to myself. If I don't happen to like a rose being considered because of its hue, I pretend it's another shade. I even considered wearing rose-colored glasses while scoring entries for form, substance, or flowering effect.

As my garden progressed through its two-year demonstration status, so did the proximity of my scores to those of the big guys. Last November, all of the roses that won were in my top ten, too, though not necessarily at the top. In fact, the rose that grabbed my heart won't even be declared All-America, although it will be introduced to commerce.

That's the American process for you.

Roses from Hell

At the beginning of last year's rose season, a young woman visited my garden claiming that she wanted help in selecting three modern rosebushes.

"Do you already have an idea what you want to grow?" I asked.

"Well," she responded hesitantly, "I've been told to consider 'Tropicana', 'Sterling Silver', and 'Chrysler Imperial'."

Just before asking if Satan himself had suggested that ludicrous trio from hell, I resolved instead to change her mind.

'Tropicana' was hybridized by Germany's indefatigable rose breeder Mathias Tantau and introduced in 1960. The result of years of cross-pollination, 'Tropicana' was the very first pure orange Hybrid Tea rose, and whatever else it is, 'Tropicana' is undeniably orange! Its garish color, however, is only one of its problems.

Apart from its bloom, which I find downright dumpy, the bush of 'Tropicana' is a mess. During those years I bothered to grow it, new canes appeared only every third year, so I coddled bushes with wood that looked way past its prime. Besides that, foliage not only mildewed and rusted, but 'Tropicana' is the only variety that ever black-spotted on me.

I realize that detecting fragrance in a rose is often like finding beauty in a person's face—it depends on who's doing the looking, or in this case, the smelling. Some swear 'Tropicana' is fragrant, but even when I sniff to the point of hyperventilation, I detect not a trace of scent. To 'Tropicana', I say no, never.

By introducing mauve to modern roses, the United States' Gladys Fisher, who hybridized 'Sterling Silver' in 1957, became one of the most important women in rosedom since Empress Josephine (the greatest rose benefactress ever). Since then, mauve roses have progressed to the point that rosarians in the know no longer consider the stingy 'Sterling Silver' a contender. The American Rose Society, in their 10-point scale for rating roses, now rates it at 4.5 (lower than 6.0 is "of questionable value"). I'd rate 'Sterling Silver' even lower and gave it the heave-ho years ago.

'Chrysler Imperial' has stayed around because of its catchy, classy name. It deserved its selection as an All-America rose in 1953, after which it became the red rose to beat, and beaten it was—soundly, by 'Precious Platinum', 'Toro', and 'Olympiad', to name only three.

I admit that 'Chrysler Imperial' is sumptuously fragrant, but that's about it. On the downside, there's mildew on already-dull foliage, lack of vigor, and short stems. Finally, it blues as it ages more than any red rose I know. I traded in my 'Chrysler' more than a decade ago.

I didn't relate all this dreary news to the visitor in search of advice because I didn't want her to leave my garden believing that rosarians were crotchety fussbudgets. Instead, I led her to finer roses in the same hues as the varieties she mistakenly imagined she wanted.

Rather than 'Tropicana' I talked her into 'Touch of Class'. Although I don't care for its elitist name and resent its lack of scent, I'm crazy about 'Touch of Class' and marvel at the way it changes from light orange to soft pink as its beautifully formed blossoms mature.

Getting my visitor over 'Sterling Silver' was accomplished with a single whiff of the divinely perfumed 'Angel Face'—the fetching mauve granddaughter of 'Sterling Silver'. Forgetting 'Chrysler Imperial' was easy, too—the handsome 'Mister Lincoln' (also decadently perfumed) handily took care of that burgundy-red substitution.

At the end of the growing season, my visitor called to tell me how pleased she was with her glorious trio of rose-bushes. "Whatever do you suppose made me think I wanted those duds I first asked you about?" she inquired.

"Oh, probably their notorious names," I answered.

But I still think it was the devil.

Futuristic Roses

I grew up with a mother who declared that she had "no intentions whatsoever of growing something that has more ailments named for it than any other flower." In all fairness, I reluctantly admit that roses do pose certain recurring troubles. Still, the rewards easily compensate for all efforts. For those of you who are as ornery as my mother, however, I have good news: Hybridizers are hard at work creating everblooming rose varieties that are not only revolutionary in their resistance to disease, but require only occasional pruning (some varieties might need none at all).

Rosedom is so thrilled over the development of these new beauties that no one has decreed what they should be called; some people refer to them as Modern Shrub roses—a name that probably won't stick because it's too easily confused with Heritage Shrub roses. More likely, and my personal vote, these breakthroughs will be labeled Landscape roses.

The first Landscape rose that made the gardening world sit up and take notice was 'Bonica', which grows on 5-by-5-foot plants and produces armloads of lightly scented, pale-pink flowers in clusters on gracefully arching stems. Because 'Bonica' was named an All-America rose in 1987, I recognized that it was a rose worth watching and planted several bushes. Since I still had tunnel vision in those days, attracted only by upright bushes that produced roses on long cutting stems, two years later, I yanked it out of the ground. One bush looked particularly healthy, however, almost as though it pleaded to grow in my garden. Just as I was taking it to the pile of other bushes I intended to give away (I never trash rosebushes just because they've fallen out of my picky favor), I noticed a large hollow stump with nothing growing in it and planted this lone 'Bonica' there. That was three years ago. Since, I've never sprayed the bush, nor have I taken my loppers to it at pruning time. Today, it's a mighty sight to behold and all summer long, visitors skid to a halt as they approach it. I've learned, of course, that there's more to a rosebush than roses themselves and landscape contributions are equal in importance to bouquets.

Four years after the debut of 'Bonica', another Land-scape rose won the coveted All-America title—'Carefree Wonder'—a carefree bush indeed, that's more rounded than 'Bonica', decidedly disease-resistant, and blessed with shocking-pink blossoms whose petals have a creamy reverse. Some diehard enthusiasts of modern roses complain that the blooms of 'Carefree Wonder' don't display the high-pointed centers associated with prissy Hybrid Teas, but most gardeners consider this a small price to pay for such a trouble-free rosebush. Next year, a brand-new Landscape rose will make the All-America Selections list—'All That Jazz'—another 5-by-5 plant that produces single, fully petaled coral blossoms with golden-yellow stamens.

Not all Landscape roses are All-Americas, of course. Those in the Meidiland series (pronounced *may-d-land*), from the House of Meilland (the same hybridizing clan that gave the rose world 'Peace'), weren't even entered in the All-America trials, so eager were the hybridizers to show off their introductions. So far, all with the surname of Meidiland, five varieties have been introduced by color— white, pink, scarlet, red, pearl (blush pink), and alba (white, and a terrific ground cover).

More fine Landscape roses are coming our way; I know because in my own All-American Rose Test Garden I have seen for myself the roses being considered for prestigious honors to be awarded in the next two years. Take my word, some winners are headed down the pike—varieties that are sure to alter the ways of those who still complain that roses are too much trouble. I think these newcomers might have changed even my mother's mind.

I Have Seen the Rose
of the Future, and
It's Striped

∽

My hardheaded friend Stella despises striped roses. "Stripes belong on some other flower," she says, "not roses. I won't have them in my garden." Although I've never been exactly gaga over them myself, I must admit that certain striped roses are knockouts.

'Rosa Mundi' may be the world's favorite striped rose, and it's certainly the oldest. A sport (spontaneous mutation) of the ancient *Rosa gallica officinalis,* commonly known as the apothecary rose, 'Rosa Mundi' blossoms with petals that are blush-white striped randomly with crimson, pink, and light purple, no two alike.

'Camaieux', also an ancient Gallica, is considered to be one of the most elegantly striped beauties in all of rosedom. Not only are its creamy-white petals madly splashed crimson, then purple, then lilac, the blossoms never lose fragrance as they age.

As new families of roses developed, striped roses went in and out of vogue. Then, in the nineteenth century, when Bourbon roses were introduced, striped roses became the epitome of fashion. As a special plus, unlike dowager rose varieties, Bourbons blossom more than once each season. Of the twenty-something striped Bourbon roses available in commerce, two head the pack.

'Honorine De Brabant' is the most softly striped member of the Bourbon clan, with large baby-pink blossoms streaked with soft shades of lilac and mauve. Honorine is a particularly good repeat bloomer, and blossoms are often most beautiful in fall, when sunlight isn't so harsh that colors bleach.

'Variegata Di Bologna', a relative newcomer to the Bourbon family, is the only member of Italian heritage, having been hybridized by A. Bonfiglioli in 1909. Blossoms are basically creamy white, but they are dramatically striped with crimson and purple, each one differently. Globular at first, blooms eventually flatten and quarter, remaining fragrant all the while.

Shortly after 1867, when the world was graced with the first Hybrid Tea rose, striped roses began appearing in great numbers. Although they've enjoyed only occasional bouts of popularity during this century, in the last three years, striped roses have again come into vogue, thanks in large part to Southern California's talented hybridizer Jack Christensen, who, in 1991, graced rosedom with two stunning Floribunda roses. Both have Tiger in their name.

'Tiger Tail' blossoms with sprays of flowers that are deep orange with random stripes of white or cream. Although plants are relatively short, they're bushy and sport glossy disease-resistant foliage. Alas, 'Tiger Tail' hasn't a whiff of fragrance.

'Purple Tiger', on the other hand, is plenty fragrant; it's also more dramatically colored—deep purple with flecks and stripes of white and mauve pink. Those merits alone explain the enormous success of 'Purple Tiger'. As another bonus, plants are easy to grow and low on thorns.

As far as I'm concerned, more exciting than any striped rose to date is one currently in the All-America Rose Selection process for a possible award in 1997. This yet-unnamed test rose will surely be introduced to commerce whether or not it actually wins the coveted award. I also predict that it will serve as a great arbiter for the ongoing feud between rosarians devoted to old-fashioned garden roses and those fond of modern hybrids. That's because it possesses attributes dear to both camps—it looks like an old rose but blossoms like a voracious modern upstart.

Besides all that, this hotshot Floribunda is uniquely colored. Petals are deep hot-pink shaded rose, splashed with creamy to pure-white random striations. To cap off the entire affair, fragrance is strong and the handsome deep green foliage is impervious to disease.

I'm considering ordering a bareroot bush for my friend Stubborn Stella; this doozy may just change her attitude toward striped roses.

Even Roses Get
the Blues

∽

Since genetic engineers assure us that a blue rose is just around the corner, I've been asking people what they'll think of such a find. "Oh, I don't expect to like a blue rose," most folks say, shaking their heads. "It's unnatural."

Natural or not, any fool would trade his left toe for a blue rose—it's worth a potential fortune. Worldwide, 25 billion dollars are spent on cut flowers annually, one fifth of that on roses. Fancy blossoms sell for up to ten dollars per stem. A blue rose is predicted to fetch twenty.

What worries me is not the marketability of a blue rose, but rather its precise color. Excited over synthesizing delphinidin (the pigment in petunias that turns their petals blue), scientists are eager to transfer the gene to roses, but I've never seen a truly blue petunia, only deep lavender or bluish purple. It seems to me that researchers should be fiddling with delphiniums, irises, morning glories, or lobelias—flowers that are inarguably blue.

I worry, too, that the blue darling might not hold its color, since even the gene isolators point out that delphinidin can go either red or blue depending on the pH of the soil in which plants grow. Red flowers like to sink the roots of their plants in alkaline soil, whereas plants that bloom blue prefer acidic conditions. Roses, however, have a decided preference for neutral soil. Would you care to alter the pH of an entire rose bed just to satisfy one of its inhabitants? Neither would I.

I predict that the road to an honestly blue rose will take the same route already paved by orange or mauve roses—two hues among modern roses that didn't meet with immediate success. 'Tropicana', for instance, was the first Hybrid Tea rose that carried pelargonidin, the pigment found in orange flowers. No one argues whether or not 'Tropicana' is orange, only if they care to blink often enough to tolerate its garish color. Once rose breeders got their mitts on 'Tropicana', however, they toned down its offspring to tasteful hues. Varieties such as 'Shreveport', 'Anabell', and 'Touch of Class'—all classified as orange—are ever so much easier on the eyes than 'Tropicana' is. Similarly, 'Sterling Silver' was the first mauve Hybrid Tea rose, but its many offspring are so superior that it should now be illegal to propagate the mauve forerunner.

Such disappointing histories among hybridized roses should not, however, alter the efforts of researchers determined to unveil a blue rose. Quite the contrary, I believe they should forge ahead even if they discover only a near-blue rose; it would at least be a start. Although it may prove to be a stingy bloomer on a disease-prone bush, it can be turned over to hybridizers who know just what to do to eliminate such nuisances, just as they did for 'Tropicana' and 'Sterling Silver'.

What thrills me more than the prospect of a blue rose, even one the color of lapis (which the smart money is on), is the second goal of plantsmen obsessed with genetic engineering—to extend the vase life of cut flowers. These clever folk say that blossoms wither and die because of ethylene, a compound that shortens their life. To halt the premature effects of ethylene, scientists claim, antisense compounds must be employed. Originally developed for medical applications, antisense compounds have already proven to effectively prolong the vase life of carnations. Although the task will be tougher for woody-stemmed flowers such as roses (compared to herbaceous, fleshy-stemmed plants such as carnations), I'm sure the researchers can bring it off. After all, if science can turn rose blossoms blue, it can surely prolong their lives.

Beautiful Bareroots

I bought no bareroot bushes the first year I grew roses.
First, there weren't many choices left among varieties by
the time I went shopping; but more important, I worried
that bareroot plants would never amount to much. "Looks
like a fistful of sticks to me," I'd say as I walked past bare-
roots in nursery bins. "Give me a plant in a proper pot any
day. Look, there are some rosebushes in biodegradable containers." Sold.

By the next buying season, I had become seriously
smitten with rose fever. Rosarians I liked to pal around
with took me aside to assure me that I had to get over this
aversion to naked bushes. "Get real," they urged me, "bare-
roots are the way to go." I'm so pleased that I conquered
my fear of leafless plants. You will be, too, if you give bare-
roots a try.

First, appealing to your practical side, bareroot plants
are cheaper than those already potted up, not just because
of the cost of the pot and soil, but also because of the labor
of proper planting. Often, vigorous roses get planted in
containers too small to accommodate their roots, which get

crammed inside. Bareroot bushes, on the other hand, slip into holes especially dug for them, allowing the luxury of spreading roots precisely where they want to settle. Finally, roses planted from containers need time to readjust to the soil in their new home after they have been removed from their cans or grow through biodegradable containers. Bareroot plants, on the contrary, start life in homes with soil prepared just for them.

If you're at all leaning toward planting roses bareroot, your next step should be in the direction of catalogs, preferably from suppliers who specialize in roses. Before you read the first page of these wickedly winning publications, however, keep in mind that their writers are out to sell. Nursery owners don't admit that a particular rose is prone to mildew because they'd just as soon not talk about it; neither do tradespeople bother to mention when varieties are stingy— just look at the pretty picture, please. And, if you're after perfume, beware of any rose described as "lightly fragrant"; only bloodhounds know for sure.

Once you decide to order, you must specify grade. Whenever possible, always buy grade 1 bushes—plants that have been field grown for two years and have at least three vigorous canes (main stems). If you finally spot that rose you've been coveting and learn that it's now available only in grade 1½, I say go for it—canes will be fewer and plants decidedly smaller than grade 1, but next season, you'll be a year ahead of the game. Never buy grade 2 or those wax-coated, packaged rose plants in supermarkets (they're dry, never guaranteed as to variety, and it takes a blowtorch to melt the wax).

As for which rose varieties to choose, that, of course, depends on what appeals to you. Once you know that you want, say, a red rose rich in perfume or a climber that will gobble up an unsightly shed, ask a local rosarian which varieties perform well where you garden; with roses, you can't beat local talent.

If you read how a rose like 'White Masterpiece' has taken Phoenix by storm, don't be tempted to order it unless you, too, garden where temperatures are hot enough to coax its heavily petaled blooms to open properly. Assuming you want a white rose and live where summers are mild, local experts will probably advise planting 'Pascali' or 'Sheer Bliss', both of which have far fewer petals.

If you crave to grow roses hot off the hybridizing bench, after learning how they perform locally, have a look at next year's All-America Rose Selections. Better yet, visit your closest municipal rose garden and see for yourself which roses shine regardless of their age. But whatever else you do, if you decide on roses for next season, give bareroot bushes a try. Once you witness the miracle of how these fistfuls of sticks mature, you'll never buy roses any other way.

Secondhand Rose

A friend called recently to say that she was terribly embarrassed that she didn't know the proper answer to a question about her roses. "In the middle of a cocktail party, some smarty-pants asked if my roses grew on their own roots," she said indignantly. "I wanted to ask 'who else,' but I didn't dare—he seemed like the kind of person who knew what he was talking about."

I explained to my friend that the correct answer to the question was, no, that her roses were budded onto rootstock. When she asked how I was certain of that, I explained that I knew she bought them from a nursery that sells only budded roses. "Besides," I continued, "the oldest rose in your garden is 'America', which was hybridized in 1976, and roses are protected under patent laws for seventeen years, during which time it's illegal to propagate them asexually."

"This is getting heavy," she responded, "we better talk it out over lunch."

Budded roses, which make up more than 95 percent of roses in commerce, are grafted onto rootstock—that portion of a rosebush that remains underground. Rootstock comes from older rose varieties known not for their blooms, which are usually insignificant, even ugly, but rather for their capacity for rapid massive root development.

Roses on their own roots grow from cuttings. Although it takes longer to grow rosebushes from cuttings, advocates of own-root roses believe such rosebushes are worth the wait. First, roses growing on their own roots are virus free. Rose propagators have been plagued for years with rootstock infected with virus impossible to eradicate except with heat so intense that entire plants are sacrificed. If present, virus in the rootstock is eventually transmitted to the hybrid, rendering it unsightly. Second, because they grow on their own roots, roses taken from cuttings don't develop suckers. Finally, own-root roses are said to be more winter-hardy and to enjoy a longer life than budded roses.

If you want to try rooting your own roses, first select varieties from which you can realistically expect success. Almost all roses known as old garden roses root well, particularly members of the Gallica, Damask, and Rugosa families. Next, take cuttings from established rosebushes either during spring or fall, when plant cells within rose wood are most active. Supple stems terminating in buds just beginning to show color should be harvested from their bushes with at least four budding eyes—swellings that signal new growth. Remove all but the uppermost set of leaflets.

A good rooting medium is composed equally of sand, peat moss, and perlite. Tips of cuttings should be dipped in a rooting stimulant (liquid seems better than powder), and inserted into the rooting soil with two eyes below and two above. Cuttings should then be placed in an area of 50 percent shade and kept moist with frequent misting.

If you've fallen in love with a rose that's no longer in commerce, try rooting it yourself. It's also wise to take more cuttings than you intend to plant, thereby increasing your chances that at least one of them will form a sturdy root system.

Among modern roses, the more vigorous the hybrid, the greater are its chances for growing on its own roots. The majestic Grandiflora 'Queen Elizabeth', for instance, grows well on its own roots, whereas the relatively puny 'White Lightnin'' Grandiflora won't budge unless grafted onto vigorous rootstock. Similarly, the aggressive Floribunda 'Seapearl' has a better chance of growing on its own roots than does the diminutive 'Angel Face'.

Try rooting any modern hybrid you like, but remember that roses are protected under patent for seventeen years. If you intend to enjoy a rosebush that you root yourself, then have it, but never try to peddle it.

Rambling Roses Bloom
Only Once. So What?

Although it's acceptable to interchange the words *climbing* and *rambling* when discussing most garden plants, it's a mistake to do so with roses. Climbing roses blossom intermittently all summer long, but Rambling roses bloom only once.

Rambling roses are unrivaled in their ability to shower plants with blossoms from bottom to top. With some varieties, blossoming lasts two months; others bloom only half that long. Still, it doesn't seem to matter. As mentioned by Christopher Warner (Britain's wizard of Rambling roses) while discussing the coppery-pink 'Albertine', "It is perhaps surprising that a rose that has only three weeks of bloom should have remained so long a favorite." Obviously, it says something about the quality of the bloom, regardless of how long the show lasts. After a few seasons, the fact that ramblers blossom only once each year is rendered incidental.

Gardeners' favoritism for ramblers has doubtlessly developed because no other rose can so thoroughly camouflage an entire rickety roof or engulf a dead stump. Some ramblers grow well in trees (particularly deciduous ones so that coexistence can be arbitrated at pruning time). Grown into trees, blossoms show to their best advantage because they can be viewed from below—always their best angle.

Although there is a host of them to choose from, certain varieties deserve special mention. First, the four varieties that make up the Banksia family. The Banksias are those roses generally referred to as house eaters because they quickly scramble over entire roofs and fill whole trees. Alas, they aren't particularly hardy, but if the temperature in your garden doesn't dip below 20° F. for longer than five successive nights, you can probably grow mighty Banksias. *R. Banksiae* 'Banksiae' is the most strongly perfumed member of the family and produces flowers that are less than 1 inch wide, but are fully petaled, pure white, and rosettes shaped. *R. Banksiae* 'Lutea' is a carbon copy of *R. Banksiae* 'Banksiae' except that it's deep to pale yellow. Then, there are two Banksias whose blossoms are single rather than double. *R. Banksiae* 'Lutescens' is bright yellow and *R. Banksiae* 'Normalis' (thought to be the oldest of the clan) is snow white.

Three pungently fragrant creamy-white ramblers from Europe know no bounds when it comes to spread. 'Bobbie James', 'Kiftsgate', and 'Rambling Rector' have all been responsible for toppling trees and collapsing garden sheds under their mature weight.

If you've ever visited the Roseraie de l'Hay in Paris during May or June, you've seen 'Alexander Girault' in its glory; the rose was planted to smother a majestic lattice framework that frames the center of the garden of heirloom roses. Not everyone is crazy about the color of the blossoms of 'Alexander Girault' (reddish-salmon petals around green button eyes), but no one quarrels with its fragrance or graceful growing habits.

It strikes me as odd that I had to travel to England to meet a rose that was not only born in America but also named for the founder of the famous nursery Roses of Yesterday and Today, in Watsonville, California. The single flowers of 'Francis E. Lester' that form in large trusses, start out clear pink but fade to white, resembling apple blossoms but smelling like fruit compote. Foliage is tapered, long, and glossy green.

A rose buddy of mine has a lovely home two hours south of London. Although she loves roses of every age and growth habit, her pets are the ramblers that surround the house. When I got a load of Mr. Lester in full bloom, I literally stopped in my tracks. So will you when you see a contented Rambling rose strutting its stuff.

Maybe it's just as well that Rambling roses bloom only once each year; I'm not sure I'm up to the experience more often.

Nothing Standard
About Tree Roses

∞

W hen most gardeners think of roses in the garden, they imagine bushes, shrubs, or climbers. In so doing, they overlook one of the very nicest ways to grow roses—as standards. Also known as tree roses, standards are actually a combination of three separate rose varieties—the one that is to bloom, the shank, and the rootstock.

The shank, the sole purpose of which is to provide height for the hybrid growing on top, comes from varieties of roses known for producing long, arching canes. When harvested, all side growth is removed and any subsequent sprouts are rubbed off. The rootstock of choice is the same as that for bush or shrub roses—a variety known to quickly establish sizable root systems. Rootstock comes from rose varieties known not for their blooms, which are usually insignificant, but rather for their capacity for massive root development.

Although conventional rosebushes have one graft uniting the hybrid to the rootstock, standards have two (the shank is budded to the hybrid at one end and to the rootstock at the other).

Standards sold in nurseries are usually between 18 inches to 3 feet tall, even taller if custom budded (I have a 10-footer, staked to within an inch of its life). Standards are what landscaper's dreams are made of, especially as a means of squeezing in additional roses. Since their major growth will be carried so high, tree roses can be planted smack between mature bushes. Standards are also popular for lining walkways and paths, particularly when handsome, low-growing companions are planted at their feet.

Be careful when choosing rose varieties to grow as standards. Although theoretically any rose can be grown as a standard, aggressive varieties such as the majestic Grandifloras 'Queen Elizabeth' and 'Gold Medal' are ultimately disappointing—they become top-heavy, and overstaking looks crude.

Certain Hybrid Teas grow well as standards; 'Bewitched', for instance. Although the clear-pink, intensely fragrant blossoms of 'Bewitched' border on being oversized, the bush on which they flower is modest. The same is true for other Hybrid Teas such as 'Pascali', 'Duet', and 'Just Joey', but not some—'Honor', 'Sheer Bliss', and 'Brandy', all of which are too vigorous to grow as tree roses.

Rambling and shrub roses that have a natural weeping growth habit, such as 'Excelsa' and 'Nozomi', are ideal, as are many Miniature roses. Best of all, however, are Floribundas.

Floribunda (literally, *an abundance of flowers*) roses produce clusters of blossoms in relatively short-stemmed sprays.

Like their stems, bushes of Floribundas are low growers and naturally form bushy plant habits, making them ideal for standards.

Depending on your color preference, there are numerous Floribundas from which to choose. If you like red (specifically, ruby red), 'Europeana' grows into a comely standard rose. Blossoms are shaped like rosettes and appear above handsome foliage that remains mahogany red until just before blooms appear, when it turns emerald green.

If white appeals to you (especially off-white shades sometimes called "champagne"), ask your nursery if they cultivate 'French Lace' as a standard. If so, buy it.

Mauve is nicely represented with 'Angel Face', a ruffly affair with perfume-packed petals surrounding a cluster of golden-yellow stamens. Standards of 'Angel Face' mature into plump bushes that look perfectly at home when grown as a standard.

My personal favorite among Floribunda tree roses is 'Summer Fashion', an irresistible blend of pink and yellowish white. Blooms of 'Summer Fashion' are stunners, whether they occur one to a stem or in moderately sized sprays.

Standard roses, which are ideal for growing in biodegradable containers, look terrific in containers on sundecks or patios, so you can purchase them anytime during the year. Now, for example.

Smothering the Ground
with Roses

When gardeners discuss ground covers, they usually mention plants that either quickly form lush carpets of green, such as vinca and sweet woodruff, or plants that actually like being walked on, such as chamomile. Rarely, however, do roses spring to mind when rattling off names of favorite ground covers—a pity, since several varieties of roses nicely hug the ground.

Before considering using a rose to camouflage an unsightly slope, be forewarned that, in spite of their name, ground cover roses don't appreciate being trampled. You'll figure this out for yourself if you ever try walking on these roses without sturdy boots, because many of the best varieties have vicious thorns.

The two most famous ground cover roses bloom only each spring. 'Max Graf' is so vigorous and oblivious to the soil in which it's planted that it aggressively gobbles up entire sand dunes. Although it rarely grows taller than 2 feet, 'Max Graf' sends out long shoots that root themselves to travel farther. Blossoms are single, pale pink, and smell like a heady fruit compote.

'Raubritter', which matures into a low-spreading mound, is a favorite ground cover rose in Europe but has only recently caught on in America. Because of their deeply cupped formation, its mildly fragrant, mid-pink, nonrecurring blossoms resemble those of old roses and are formed all along the length of thorny branches with dark green, wrinkled, leathery foliage. If mildew is no stranger to your garden, read on, because 'Raubritter' has an annoying affinity with powdery mildew.

'Ferdy', on the other hand, is remarkably disease resistant, although it's tall for a ground cover (to 3 feet). A plump lad, 'Ferdy' grows at least twice as wide as he does tall. Salmon-pink blossoms appearing in clusters in early summer and again in fall are scentless but profuse.

If perfume is what you're after, consider 'Fairyland', which grows no taller than 2 feet but twice as broad, and produces scads of small, rosy-pink, strongly fragrant blossoms. 'Fairyland' is also notoriously hardy in areas where winters are cruel.

A Dutch hybridizer named Ilsink introduced two ground cover roses that are taking Europe by storm. 'Red Blanket' grows twice as wide as it does tall and blossoms repeatedly with clusters of small, semidouble, rose-red, faintly fragrant flowers. 'Smarty', the half sister of 'Red Blanket' (they share one parent), blooms with sprays of seven-petaled baby-pink blossoms that emit a fruity fragrance.

'Nozomi', often listed as a Climbing Miniature rose, also makes a fine ground cover, particularly in rock gardens. Trusses of flat, slightly fragrant, pearl-pink blossoms appear in midsummer against small glossy foliage. Although it rarely grows over 1 foot tall, Nozomi spreads to 5 feet. If you admire 'Nozomi', and I can't imagine why you wouldn't, you should also know that it makes the quintessential weeping standard (rose tree).

'Ralph's Creeper', named in honor of the indefatigable American Miniature rose hybridizer Ralph Moore of Visalia, California, is a fine choice for those who want to cover their ground with small bright-red blossoms with white eyes. Plants are particularly vigorous and disease resistant as well.

There are several terrific ground cover roses headed down the pike. I'm growing one variety under consideration for an All-America rose award in 1996 that's a doozy—to 6 feet in all directions after only one year in the ground. Although the five-petaled, blinding-red, golden-eyed blossoms might not be to everyone's taste, the glossy, emerald-green ironclad foliage is bound to please.

Like many of its ancestors, this yet-to-be-named contender produces abundant thorns that must be reckoned with; they'll snare any pant leg nearby. But that doesn't matter—you won't walk on the plants, you'll merely allow them to smother your ground.

Let Your Fingers Do
the Pruning

∽

In the giddiness of spring, well-grown rosebushes of modern hybrids optimistically sprout more new growth than they can realistically support. The remedy, nipping in the bud, requires no equipment other than your fingers. Finger pruning also assures that gardeners get the precise blooms they had in mind.

Tender rose growth is so supple that you won't need tools to remove it; just rub it off with your thumb. Begin at the tops of bushes by inspecting new growth on laterals (rose wood emanating from main canes). Laterals often require discipline because they're capable of sprouting buds along their entire lengths. Begin rubbing out new growth by sacrificing anything growing toward the center of the bush. Ultimately, because of limited space and poor circulation, interior growth produces shredded blossoms or diseased foliage.

In the same way, rub off new growth at the heart of the rosebush—the bud union, where the base of the bush has become globular from the graft of a modern hybrid onto vigorous rootstock. It is from this landmark that important new growth stems.

By spring, the average modern rosebush has been pruned of all but six or seven main canes (vigorous Grandifloras may be left with more, and diminutive Floribundas with fewer). Then, warmed by spring sun, bud unions swell and sprout multiple red nubs that develop into new canes. If you're after long-stemmed large flowers, you have no choice but to curtail exuberance.

Bud unions of healthy rosebushes may well sprout a dozen new canes during the first month of spring. That's too many; rub off half of them. First, rub off any budding eyes growing in the middle of the bush. Next, try to anticipate whether those you leave will interfere with others as they grow. If you think everything will not be able to coexist, rub off more.

I've never understood why many gardeners tremble in front of rosebushes that need to be disbudded. Disbudding is nothing more than the sacrifice of certain rosebuds in return for majestic maturity of others. A dutiful disbudder simply declares a preference for either one-to-a-stem blooms or sprays of blossoms.

One-to-a-stem disbudding is mostly for Hybrid Teas. Some roses produce only one bud per stem, as if they know that's how they're prettiest. Others produce one large bud at the end of a stem and usually two smaller buds just beneath.

The terminal bud is the large one and you want to leave it. Side buds should be removed when they get to be about ¼ inch long. At that length, they can be grasped at the base and snapped off close to the stem without leaving a stub. Be sure to hold on to the terminal bud when you make these succulent snaps; you wouldn't want to end up with it in the palm of your hand. No matter what you do, the terminal bud will continue to develop and open long before weaker side buds. Take side buds out early and direct all energy to the terminal bud. If you're thinking about as much bloom as possible after you cut and want to leave side buds, forget it; they'll never open once they're off the bush.

However, if you're disbudding to produce sprays rather than a single blossom per stem, the technique is the opposite. In order for all energy to be channeled into spray formation, terminal buds are removed and side buds are left to develop.

Generally, Hybrid Tea roses are disbudded for one-to-a-stem blooms and Floribundas and Grandifloras are disbudded for sprays. You might experiment with reversing the disbudding procedures, if for no other reason than to satisfy yourself about which looks better. You may decide that you like some Hybrid Teas in sprays and certain Floribundas or Grandifloras one to a stem.

Your call.

A Rose Named Rayford

A recent visitor to my rose garden asked when I thought a rose would be named for me.

"Oh, I don't think I'd let that happen," I replied.

"Why in the world not?" she asked, looking at me as though I should be ashamed for appearing so ungrateful.

I went on to explain to my well-intended guest that I simply didn't care to let an inferior rose bear my name, the way other rose lovers have.

Of all the roses named for famous Americans, not one of them (the flowers, not the citizens) is thought better than fair by avid rosarians across the United States who vote on these things every three years. They include 'Amy Vanderbilt', 'Arlene Francis', 'Audie Murphy', 'Bing Crosby', 'Ginger Rogers', 'Helen Hayes', 'Helen Traubel', 'Mrs. Luther Burbank', and 'Peggy Lee'.

Some roses have been named for presidents. If you ask a Democrat to name one, he'll sing the praises of 'John F. Kennedy'. So will I, but only to a point. JFK (as it's known to rosarians) produces greenish-white, stiffly perfect blossoms, but its bush lacks vigor and its blooms are scentless.

Rose-growing Republicans in the know won't even discuss 'President Herbert Hoover'—it's thought to be of questionable value by the pros because of its puny bush. There once grew a rose named 'Richard Nixon', but it was yanked from nursery bins right after Watergate.

First ladies have fared no better. So many different roses are called 'Martha Washington' that no one's even sure what color she really is. 'Rosalyn Carter' is about to be dropped from commerce for lack of vigor; 'Lady Bird Johnson' surely will be; and the days are clearly numbered for 'First Lady Nancy'.

Something is wrong with every single rose named for a state. 'Alabama' has a weak neck and its blossoms droop; blooms of 'Arizona' are too often formless; and 'Arkansas' is an unappealing muddy orange. Like the state itself, 'Louisiana' mildews; and 'Oklahoma' is just too stingy.

Maybe what I should do if I really want a rose named after me is to butter up those hybridizers who are still working on creating new varieties from antique parents. Several of the roses called old garden roses are beauties. 'Madame Hardy', for instance, which was hybridized in France in 1832 and named for the wife of the head gardener to Empress Josephine (a passionate rosarian), is considered to be one of the finest Damask roses ever created. Similarly, 'Fantin Latour' is thought to be an exemplary Centifolia rose and 'Madame Isaac Perriere' is a queen among Bourbon roses. One of the best of the Portland roses is named 'Jacques

Cartier' and a favorite among Hybrid Perpetual roses is called 'Baronne Prevost'. Then, of course, there's the lovely Noisette rose 'Madame Alfred Carrière', and the ubiquitous Polyantha 'Cecile Brunner'.

This idea isn't as far-fetched as it seems, since old garden roses are being hybridized every day. Breeders simply choose antique parents and cross their pollen. As long as they stick with dowager mothers and elderly fathers, hybridizers will always be able to create new old roses.

I have high standards for a rose to which I'd lend my name. First, I'd like an ironclad shrub that's impervious to mildew, rust, and black spot, and ignored by munching insects. Second, this hell-bent-for-survival bloom factory should produce nonstop blossoms from early summer to late fall. Finally, the flowers must be packed with perfume. Oh yes, golden-apricot blooms would be nice (yellow is the most elusive color to rose hybridizers).

In view of such lofty ideals, I fear, if I'm ever to have a namesake, I'll have to hybridize it myself. Face it, if someone else does, would they name it Rayford? I don't think so.

PART 5

Gardening
for Fragrance

Whose Nose Knows?

W hen it comes to discussing fragrance in flowers, nothing is clearer than the need to establish ground rules. Although gardeners seldom concur on precisely how to describe a particular fragrance, everyone agrees that some flowers smell enough alike to be loosely grouped together.

No expert has done more to introduce order into the classification of fragrance than Roy Genders, a fine British horticulturist who specialized in herbs and rare perennials. According to Genders, perfumed blossoms should be classed according to the predominate chemical substances in their essential oils. Using this approach, he established ten divisions. Two of these, however, have little appeal: the indoloid group, which has flowers that smell like decaying meat or fish, and the aminoid group, whose blossoms reek of ammonia. The remaining eight divisions—heavy, aromatic, violet, rose, lemon, fruit, animal, and honey—are worthy of unending praise.

Flowers in the heavy group contain the potentially obnoxious indole, but it's cut with benzyl acetate, which diffuses foul overtones. Nevertheless, if you bury your nose in your tuberose lei after you've just set foot in Hawaii, you'll detect an unmistakable hint of putrefaction. Other flowers in the heavy group include osmanthus, viburnum, lily of the valley, and honeysuckle.

Flowers in the aromatic group contain eugenol, the essential oil found in plants that smell of cinnamon, clove, vanilla, or balsam. A hint of clove, for example, is unmistakable in stock, carnation, and peony, and vanilla can be detected in sweet pea, witch hazel, acacia, and wisteria. The bittersweet fragrance of almond is present in heliotrope, flowering rush, and choisya.

Flowers in the violet group derive their fragrance from a substance called ionone. As it ages, however, ionone loses its charm and takes on the smell of damp woodland moss or freshly cut cucumbers. Even insects avoid it, which is perhaps why violets are among the few self-fertilizing flowers. Mignonette, a European favorite, is also rich in ionone.

The rose scent is not limited to roses. In fact, some members of the genus *Pelargonium* have foliage so laden with the key ingredient, an alcohol called geraniol, that their leaves are often distilled for essential oils to substitute for the costly attar of roses. Discerning noses, however, smell the difference.

Flowers in the lemon group harbor citral, unmistakable in certain China roses, waterlilies, verbenas, and the elegant *Magnolia Soulangiana*.

Fruit-scented flowers emit fragrances associated with specific fruits. Most gardeners agree that many members of the genus *Philadelphus* smell more like oranges than oranges themselves; *Iris graminea* smells like apricots; the Japanese rambler *Rosa Wichuraiana* like green apples; and the robust *Rosa Soulieana* like ripe bananas.

Musk, the most common fragrance in animal-scented plants, is often associated with Moss and Musk roses but is also present in some species of grape hyacinth.

Although several honeysuckles and escallonias smell strongly of honey, as does sweet sultan, no flowers in the honey-scented group have a more delightful perfume than various members of the genus *Buddleia,* commonly known as the butterfly bush.

If I've learned nothing else from my infatuation with fragrance, it's that one person's rose is another's stinkweed, and that not everyone can appreciate the aroma of certain plants, regardless of how they are supposed to smell. For instance, I can detect no perfume whatsoever in the brown boronia (*Boronia megastigma*), though others swoon over its aroma, which they compare to ripe peaches. I think they've fallen out of their tree—the sniffers, not the peaches.

Even though I bite my tongue, I feel only sorrow when people admit that they are immune to the scent of roses that make me dizzy with their bawdy perfume, and I remind myself of that brown boronia. Then again, when all is smelled and done, whose nose knows?

Sowing a Carpet
of Chamomile

I first saw chamomile at Vita Sackville-West's Sissing-hurst. The fragrant herb was in a 1½-by-2-foot patch beneath a bench (a wonderful perfumed resting spot for an overworked gardener). A pitiful sign said "Please Do Not Touch": Vita never had sufficient sun to grow enough chamomile for ground cover, though she often mentioned how she'd love to.

When Bob Galyean and I planted a fragrant garden, we decided to outdo Vita by planting an entire chamomile knoll. From two flats of seedlings, plugs were set 9 inches apart over a large mound in front of some magnolia and birch trees. By midsummer the knoll was blanketed with chamomile. Early that fall, Bob took plugs from the established areas and planted them near the edges of adjacent paths. They spread like gossip.

"I think we should go for broke and shoot for a whole lawn," Bob suggested, pointing to a sunny 20-foot-wide stretch of perfectly drained sandy soil between two 80-foot-long parallel rows of hawthorn trees. "Chamomile obviously likes it here." I agreed, chuckling smugly over what Vita would think of the audacious plan, and Bob began investigating growing chamomile from seed.

We had read that chamomile seeds are tiny and hard to come by. Are they ever! After two months of talking with every seeds merchant Bob could locate, he finally discovered someone who could special order seeds for a price tag just under that for rose attar. Hoping that the seeds would flourish as had their plugs of predecessors, Bob ordered 6 ounces of the tiniest seeds either of us had ever seen. In March, we tilled the would-be lawn, leveled it, and yanked every weed in sight.

Because the seeds were so fine and costly, Bob didn't dare distribute them from a conventional seed spreader. Instead, he mixed them with white river sand left over from a masonry job and gingerly broadcast the mixture off the tip of a square-nosed shovel. The area was then covered with a thin layer of nitralized sawdust that was pressed firmly into the sandy soil with a water-filled lawn roller.

What followed were three weeks of agony deciding whether sprouts were actually chamomile or unwelcome weeds. During week four, we assured ourselves that the featherlike willowy branches actually were chamomile, then weeded out all else. By the end of summer, the lawn was established. By fall it needed mowing. We've never bought another costly seed and have given plugs to everyone who asked.

Chamomile has been praised for centuries, mostly for its soothing medicinal qualities, but also as a diuretic and for preventing nightmares. Recent reports claim that an infusion of the entire plant is a spiffy hair rinse, especially for blondes.

Although there are numerous species of this useful fragrant plant, just two are in general cultivation, and only one will cover your ground. *Anthemis nobilis,* the perennial Roman chamomile, is the ground cover, whereas its German cousin, *Matricaria Chamomilla* (said to make finer tea, with an overtone of pineapple), is an upright annual. You shouldn't walk on the 3-foot-high German chamomile, but you're welcome to tromp the prostrate Italian variety. Bruised by footsteps, Roman chamomile willingly releases its earthy scent, which many gardeners claim smells like trodden apples.

If you long for chamomile because you want to brew your own tea, remember to use only the flowers and to plant in full sun where soil is poor and drainage is perfect. Then, prepare yourself for a no-nonsense fragrant delight that thrives on abuse.

I ache to show Vita our lawn.

Daphne—Watch Out, It's Addictive

If you ask a gardener devoted to fragrance to name the most persnickety plant he grows, he will very likely say daphne. But if you ask this same person to choose a favorite scent, he might say daphne again.

However difficult the plant, daphne's perfume is irresistible. Its blossoms harbor many distinct smells in one fragrance: Lemon's there, to be sure, but so are honey and roasted nutmeg. Daphne is so strong that a mere sprig of one of the more intoxicating species can scent an entire room.

The first time I discovered daphne's ravishing perfume, the hostess at a dinner party had some blossoms floating in a bowl on a side table. "That's winter daphne," she proclaimed. "Take a whiff." I was a pest at that side table for the remainder of the evening, sometimes to the point of hyperventilation.

As I'm want to do when I fall head over heels for a plant, I bought every variety of daphne I could get my hands on. That was a mistake.

Although impervious to severe winters, *Daphne Mezereum* is a pain to grow. Plants grow best from seed, which takes at least two years to germinate, after which time the species can be expected to grow a mere foot in a decade! Worst of all, *D. Mezereum* resents being cut. No thanks.

D. Cneorum, the rose daphne, should be thought of as a ground cover since plants grow three times as wide as they do tall. Known also as the garland flower, *D. Cneorum* bears sweetly scented rose-pink blossoms in clusters at the ends of branches in May, and again in August.

British horticulturist Albert Burkwood tried his hand at hybridizing daphne and hit the jackpot when he crossed *D. Cneorum* with *D. caucasica,* a deciduous shrub from the Caucasus. One promising offspring would have been reward enough, but Burkwood delivered two. The first, *D.* x *Burkwoodii,* produces clusters of fragrant white flowers around the tips of branches on a 3- to 4-foot plant.

Although pretty, and considerably less temperamental than most daphnes, I'm afraid *D.* x *Burkwoodii* is almost homely next to its ravishing sister, *D.* x *Burkwoodii* 'Somerset'. More robust than the first hybrid, Somerset gets at least 1½ feet taller and proportionately more plump. Best of all, it's the easiest daphne I know to grow.

The daphne that makes fragrance gardeners craziest of all is *D. odora* (winter daphne). The sole reason we tolerate such stubbornness is that *D. odora* is seductively perfumed—the quintessence of daphne. Why else should we tolerate such an ungrateful plant? Bushes set out into adjacent identical holes grow as though they're in different countries. After talking to numerous gardeners with similar I-can't-imagine-what-caused-that-daphne-to-die stories, I've decided that there is no easy answer. A percentage of *D. odora* seem propagated to self-destruct for no apparent reason.

Still, once you bring winter daphne to bloom, it will be worth having watered it regularly (but never too much at a time) and provided perfect drainage. Blossoms clustered in nosegays are pink to deep rose on the outside, with creamy throats. There are several cultivated varieties, including the pure-white Alba; Rose Queen, which has larger flowers than the species; and Marginata, featuring thick, narrow, glossy foliage edged in off-white.

Although I still grow several daphnes, I've given the heave-ho to pokey ones and those for which I can't snitch blossoms. Choosing between Somerset and winter daphne, however, would put me in a real pickle. Were I to base my choice only on fragrance, of course I'd take *D. odora*. For sheer beauty, Somerset would be a shoo-in.

Don't Call Pelargoniums "Geraniums"

I t's a pity that someone long ago started calling pelargonium "scented geranium." Now few gardeners can
explain the difference. *Geranium* is in fact a separate botanical genus, one far less appealing to the gardener interested
in fragrance. Just remember that anyone raving about the
fragrance of their "geranium" is really referring to that of
their pelargonium.

Pelargonium is a genus of more than two hundred species
native to South Africa. There are records that document
pelargoniums in London early in 1632, during the reign of
Charles I. For almost two centuries, however, they were
enjoyed only by those wealthy enough to afford greenhouses. It seems clear that servants in manor houses snitched
leaves to try in pots on their own windowsills, for by the
nineteenth century, pelargoniums flourished in cottages all
over Britain. Victorians lined their stairways with pots of
scented pelargoniums so that their long garments brushed
the plants and perfumed the air. In summer, the containers
were moved outdoors to line paths for the same purpose.

Few plants offer a wider array of scents than pelargoniums. The most prevalent variety is *Pelargonium graveolens,* the so-called rose geranium that is laden with geraniol, the essence of rose perfume. Other popular varieties include those that smell like lemon, orange, mint (several flavors), cinnamon, nutmeg, filbert, almond, or balsam. (I grow one variety called Tutti-frutti that somehow manages to combine several of these scents all at once.)

When you visit a nursery to purchase pelargoniums, be sure to smell what you're considering purchasing. Ask permission first, explaining that you're not picking leaves, just rubbing them to release their scent. Also, save some fingers or the back of your hand for last-minute decisions. If you squeeze indiscriminately, you'll reek of a spice rack, and you won't be able to identify what you just bruised.

Although scented pelargoniums blossom, you won't take much notice of their pretty small flowers, whether they're white, orange, or lilac to purple; it's the leaves that matter. Foliage of most varieties is large, midgreen, deeply cut, and covered in down, sometimes oily to the touch, but always fragrant.

Before you take home your first pelargonium, be forewarned that it may not last through winter, unless, of course, you live in the tropics. Although the majority of pelargoniums in commerce will stand up to light frosts, none will endure a hard freeze. Even a moderate frost may turn mature plants to a hideous shade of brown, almost overnight. If you can stand the sight, leave the dead foliage; it will help to protect the roots, which may or may not rebound in spring. Fortunately, rooting pelargoniums couldn't be easier. Slips taken at summer's end will root in plain sand, often without the help of a root stimulant. Cuttings that winter over indoors grow to maturity the following summer.

Pelargoniums thrive in any soil that drains well. Though they prefer full sun, particularly in coastal areas, pelargoniums accept some, but never full, shade. Flavor and scent increase if plants are kept on the dry side (only the top inch of the soil should be damp) and feedings should be held to a minimum (no more than two or three times a year).

Ideal as pot plants, pelargoniums flourish in containers ranging from small terra-cotta pots to wine barrels. Before transplanting to the next-largest container, keep in mind that plants perform best when their roots are slightly pot-bound.

Pelargoniums are popular among cooks for flavoring ice cream, jelly, cake, and tea. Flower arrangers like to include pelargonium leaves to ensure that bouquets smell nice, especially if nothing else in the arrangement is notably fragrant. The French distill scented pelargoniums for an inexpensive substitute for rose attar, and fair-weather gardeners bless pelargoniums for being so free of diseases and pests.

Acacias—Fragrant Yellow Powder Puffs

~

Authorities swear that there are as many as eight hundred species of the genus *Acacia,* although only about twenty varieties are widely grown in the western and southern United States. Acacias are native to areas with temperate climates—Tasmania, South Africa, and the shores of the Mediterranean, but they grow most freely today in Australia and New Zealand, where they're also known as wattles. Because of their hardiness and tolerance to drought, acacias are used to bind hillsides, for landscaping near beaches, or, if densely planted, as windbreaks. Some noble Texan had the good taste to introduce *Acacia Farnesiana* to the Lone Star State, where it now grows like a native, from Beaumont to Wichita Falls.

A. Baileyana is by far the most widely grown species in America, probably because of its unusual hardiness and rapid growth. Trees scramble to 30 feet tall with girths even greater. Leaves are feathery and bluish gray; blooms, also known as mimosa when sold as cut flowers, are actually violet-scented clusters of fluffy, yellow stamens that festoon trees during January and February.

A. dealbata is similar to *A. Baileyana,* only larger and more quickly established. In Australia, *A. dealbata* is known as the silver wattle because of its shiny gray twigs and young branches. Its flowers, also yellow and intoxicatingly scented, are formed in 6- to 9-inch panicles.

A. Farnesiana, also known as sweet acacia, was named after the Farnese Palace in Rome. It's the species praised for the production of cassia oil, used to fortify violet scents. The trees, which at maturity are shorter than the two varieties already mentioned, are deciduous and have thorny branches. Plantings perform best in alkaline soils where the thermometer never dips below 15° F. Blossoms are golden yellow and formed in tiny balls. A fully grown tree, though no taller than 10 feet, can yield up to 20 pounds of blossoms each season.

Where *A. longifolia,* also known as Sydney golden wattle, grows well, it serves abundant uses. Since it usually becomes a billowy, overgrown shrub that grows at an amazing pace, it serves as a roadside planting to protect against dust and lights of oncoming traffic. *A. longifolia* seems so oblivious to the soil in which it grows that it is planted near beaches, even those with strong prevailing winds, which simply make it thrive prostrate. Although blossoms are predictably yellow and sweetly scented, unlike the foliage of most other species, the foliage of *A. longifolia* is bright green.

A. podalyriifolia, sometimes called the pearl acacia, is happier grown as a shrub than as a loose-headed tree.

Foliage is soft gray and pleasant to feel. Blossoms borne in fluffy light-yellow balls appear earlier than do those of almost any other prevalent species.

Acacias aren't long-lived (20 to 30 years), but they're such quick growers that you can replace a toppled adult with a sapling that will grow to 20 feet in three years. You can also grow acacias quite easily from seeds (gather your own from varieties you know you like). Seeds germinate well in soakable peat pots and, once established, seedlings quickly adapt to garden spots where they are expected to flourish.

With most varieties you have a choice of treating acacias either as shrubs or as trees; they'll do as they're told. If you prune out the lead shoot, plants develop as bushes; if you remove early side growth, acacias mature into trees.

If they're watered too often, almost all acacias establish prodigious root systems that stretch over the surface of the soil. If you want to keep your sidewalks from cracking open to acacia's invasive roots, water trees infrequently, but deeply, to encourage taproots that plunge themselves deep into the ground in search of water.

Magnolias to Swoon For

M y grandmother had the largest magnolia tree in town and those creamy-white blossoms she floated in shallow bowls are fixed in my mind's eye as the biggest flowers I've ever seen. At least once each week during mid- to late summer, I was sent scurrying barefoot up grandmother's tree to pluck blooms from precarious limbs that wouldn't hold anything heavier than a seventy-pound boy. I never appreciated the importance of the task then, but I do now—magnolia blossoms are among the most divinely scented of flowers, and once you've sniffed their seductive scents, nothing else smells quite like them.

Magnolias have three convenient groupings, determined by when they bloom. Group I flowers first, as early as a warm January or as late as May (after a chilly April). Magnolias in Group I are deciduous, with blossoms preceding foliage. The stark framework of their leafless trees provides quite a dramatic setting for showy blooms.

Magnolia denudata has large, globular white flowers suffused with purple. Its fragrance is sweetly seductive, and plants bloom at an early age. *M.* x *Soulangiana* isn't as strongly scented as other varieties, but its delicate fragrance is irresistibly sophisticated—sweet, but with a definite lemon afterscent. Blooms are basically pinkish white, with purple at their bases and shaded in between. There's a variety with pure-white flowers and another with grape-purple blossoms. *M. stellata,* the star magnolia, is one of the first varieties to bloom. Flowers are off-white, star shaped, and have twelve to sixteen sweetly perfumed, narrow petals. Established plants are something between a bush and a twiggy tree. *M. stellata* doesn't take up a lot of room, and it flowers when plants are mere infants, with blooms masking all wood.

Magnolias in Group II are offbeat, with varieties such as *M. acuminata,* better known as the cucumber tree, and more valued for the shade its trees cast than for the light fragrance of its green and yellow blossoms. *M. hypoleuca* produces large, heavily fragrant, goblet-shaped blooms of light yellow with scarlet stamens, on trees reaching 100 feet. *M. macrophylla* has leaves that are 3 feet long and 1 foot wide. Also in Group II, however, is *M. sinensis,* a native of China that grows to heights of less than 15 feet and blossoms with sharply fragrant petals of pure white around scarlet stamens.

Magnolias in Group III are the evergreen varieties— those that reach magnolia's greatest heights and have the longest bloom cycles. Most flowers appear in late summer, but begin in spring and extend through fall.

M. grandiflora, the laurel magnolia, is native to the southern United States, probably Florida. It can reach 100 feet, with a spread half its height. Blooms are large, creamy white, and powerfully perfumed. *M. virginiana* is semievergreen and less lofty than *M. grandiflora,* reaching only 15 feet, but its cream-to-apricot blossoms smell like lily of the valley, only stronger.

Magnolias like to grow in full sun with their roots plunged in rich, well-drained, slightly acid soil. Never crowd magnolias; they look best with nothing growing around them. In fact, soil around the base of magnolia trees shouldn't become compacted from foot traffic. You might try a well-defined water basin or an obvious, thick mulch to keep pedestrians away.

If wind is a problem, plant magnolias near, but not against, a wall or background. This will also help show off their blooms and intricately patterned limbs.

Although I've only mentioned a handful, rest assured that the United States has nearly 100 separate species, subspecies, and cultivars of magnolias in commerce. In fact, if you see or smell a particular magnolia you like, be sure to find out its precise name—once your nose decides, that's it.

Delicious Clematis

C lematises have never been as popular in America as they are in Britain, though they're catching up. In England, you rarely see an otherwise-useless dead tree that hasn't been put to good use by providing a stump for clematis to quickly gobble up. Derived from the Greek word *klema,* vine branch, clematises cling to anything that their tendrils can grab.

Although there are more than two hundred species and subspecies of clematis in commerce (many of which haven't a whiff of perfume), if you're interested in fragrance, two head the pack: *Clematis montana* and *C. Armandii.*

C. montana is not only reputed as the most vigorous of all clematis species (it quickly grows to 20 feet or taller), it's also known for its adamant resistance to chilly winters. *C. montana* blooms only in the spring of each year, but what a spectacle! Two-inch flowers that resemble anemones start out white in bud and end up pink in bloom. Blossoms form a shimmering cascade that completely hides foliage.

Gardeners have quibbled for years over precisely how *C. montana* smells. Some say like macaroons; others, like boiling toffee. To my nose, it smells more like vanilla blended with bitter almond. No matter what you believe it smells like, be forewarned that the fragrance of *C. montana* is so strong that many people can handle the heady perfume of no more than three or four blossoms floating in a bowl.

If you want an evergreen variety to relieve the monotony of winter's deciduous stretches, by all means take a look at *C. Armandii*. When I first planted this early-spring perfume-packed variety, I was told that it grew with gusto, but mine hovered at ground level long after the deciduous varieties had taken off. Once it started stretching, however, it made up for lost time and scrambled to over 30 feet tall in less than three years.

The leaves of *C. Armandii* are up to 5 inches long and are grouped in threes. White, intensely fragrant blossoms that eventually deepen to pink also appear in sets of three, at the tip of every branch. *C. Armandii* is particularly fetching when planted over arches because both its foliage and blossoms drape gracefully. Mature plants in full flower are a sight to behold, and powerfully fragrant, too.

Though not unreasonably demanding, clematises insist on a few basics. First, they must have something to grow on right away—arbors, fences, pergolas, trees, trellises, or walls—and they prefer to be tied and staked as soon as they're planted. Second, clematises like to grow in rich, well-drained soil that is slightly acidic. Although clematises grow toward full sun, their roots must be kept cool either by planting them in the shade of what they are to scramble over or by growing a shallow-rooted ground cover on top of their roots. Finally, clematises are among the few plants that like being sunk; the tops of their root balls should be set at least 2 inches underground.

A friend of mine has managed apartments in the same five-story San Francisco Victorian for more than fifty years. Not long after she moved in, she planted fragrant clematises at the bottoms of four wide light wells that seemed to get just enough sun to make plants crane their necks for it. According to my friend, the clematises took an eternity to get above the second floor, but once they did, they quickly climbed to the roof. The plants now look like elderly wisterias, with huge, gnarled trunks. For more than a month each spring, timid tenants in fear of the bawdy clematises don't dare open their bathroom or kitchen windows. Fragrance troopers keep their windows wide open, however, swearing that they never overdose on the intoxicating perfume, even in the evening, when fragrance reaches its peak.

House-Eating Wisterias

⤫

Next to climbing roses, the wisteria is the most popular deciduous vine in the world. This is thanks to a hardiness that enables it to survive all but the cruelest of winters, great adaptability (it can be grown as a vine, tree, shrub, or bank cover), showy blooms, and luscious fragrance.

The scented varieties are natives of China, Japan, or the United States. Those from the Far East were first brought to the Western world from China in the early nineteenth century and introduced as *Glycine sinensis,* commonly called the grape-flower plant. The genus was later renamed *Wistaria* (then *Wisteria*) in honor of the American botanist Charles Wistar.

Wisterias are members of the *Leguminosae* family, as are sweet peas, which have a similar vanilla fragrance. The pea-like blooms droop in clusters called racemes. Some varieties open their flowers slowly along their racemes; others pop all at once. Colors include purple, lilac, lilac-blue, pink, and white, with all shadings in between. Early bloomers show off in April; later varieties flower into June.

Before you commit yourself to a wisteria plant, be certain of three things.

1. You want it for keeps; once it has established its massive root system, wisteria is almost impossible to eradicate.

2. You can provide strong supports for it to vine and trail over. When in full foliage near season's end, mature plants put on weight like a hungry tomcat set loose in a tropical fish store.

3. You are willing to train its aimless growth. Especially when young, these plants seem to know neither where you want them to go nor how to attach themselves. When tying young vines, remember to allow for their rapid girth expansion (expandable tape works well).

With a little help from you, robust varieties will quickly climb two stories up the side of your house, fill spaces within exterior chimneys, or march along any roof line. Wisterias are the perfect plants for pergolas, arbors, and trellises. When in bloom, they'll provide a dense screen between you and your neighbors, and an even thicker one when foliage follows. The screen will disappear, of course, when wisteria's deciduous habit forces them to shed those leaves almost overnight.

Plants that have been in your garden for only one year should be pruned only lightly, or not at all if you can live with their aimless habits for another season. During this time, their growth above ground is providing food for a well-developed root system.

After a year, you must begin pruning if you're going to have any say at all in the shape the mature vines will assume. If you're training wisteria up a post with a trellis or arbor above, try to identify the main stem and cut out all others, especially suckers that abound at the base. Usually you'll have no problem identifying the primary stem—it will be longer and noticeably thicker than the others. Sometimes it's a close call between two. If your framework will support both, leave them. If it might not, make a decision and remove one, or the whole plant may topple down. Also, cut out the weak side shoots you find growing all along the vine's length—they'll never get any stronger, always deferring to the development of their superiors.

Although you'll love the show your vines provide outdoors, you'll be dying to cut some blooms for the house. Unless you use some of the vials like those used for orchids, or weighted containers with narrow channels within them, you'll find the blooms are difficult to handle. Pick some anyway and use them as best you can. You'll have so many on the vines that no one will every miss the few you snitch for indoors.

Gardenia—The Big Bertha of Fragrance

∽

My friend Denise believed she was making a generous gesture when she commissioned a garland fashioned from 6,000 gardenia blossoms to celebrate the opening night of the opera and her twenty-third wedding anniversary.

Hardly anyone, gardener or not, is ambivalent toward gardenias. For some, gardenia's luscious scent is *it* where fragrance is concerned. For others, it's vulgar.

For southerners, especially those with warm brick walls, gardenias are a must; properly placed, they're practically carefree. Gardeners in chillier climates, however, must adore gardenias sufficiently to go to the trouble of overwintering them under glass. In southwest Louisiana and southeast Texas, near the Gulf of Mexico, gardenias grow wild in cemeteries from potted plants that rooted after being left there. In Provence, French devotees keep their gardenias in large terra-cotta pots and bring them indoors during winter. The only fact upon which all these gardeners agree is that, whatever they think of it, nothing else smells quite like the gardenia.

Although only a handful of the more than 250 species of these tender evergreen shrubs (occasionally small trees) are in general cultivation, one heads the pack—*Gardenia jasminoides* (also known as cape jasmine), with forms ranging in height from ground covers shorter than 1 foot to gargantuan bushes taller than 10 feet.

Except in China, where it grows native, G. *jasminoides* isn't modest in its needs. The soil in which it is planted must simultaneously drain quickly and retain moisture (best answered by incorporating lots of peat moss during cultivation). As with rhododendrons and azaleas, gardenias should be planted high in raised beds, and their roots shouldn't be crowded or placed where they'll have to compete for nutrients. Finally, gardenias should be fed every three weeks with an acid plant food, and regularly sprayed for aphids. Even with all this pampering, flower buds refuse to set unless the minimum temperature is a least 60° F. (even then, buds will drop if temperatures vary too widely).

Gardenia foliage is glossy, dark green, and arranged in whorls of three leaves. Heavily scented, waxlike blossoms, whether single or double, are white and up to 4 inches across.

Although there are supposedly species that emit no scent, I've never come across any; the closest I've found is G. *spathulifolia,* which grows as a small tree and produces solitary blossoms that, compared to its cousins, is only mildly scented.

The reason gardenia blossoms cause such controversy among those who smell them is the presence of indole in the chemical substance of their essential oils. Indoloid flowers such as skunk cabbage contain pure indole, rendering them thoroughly unpleasant. Gardenias, tuberoses, philadelphus, viburnum, lily of the valley, honeysuckle, and other members of the group of heavy-fragrance flowers, however, include benzylacetate and methyl anthranilate among their heady scents, both of which diffuse the potentially foul overtones of indole.

The question of how many gardenia blossoms it takes to create a cloying aroma is dictated by the size of the room in which they're placed and whether it's ventilated. In a dining room, for instance, many people float only two or three blossoms in a bowl of water, being careful never to finger the petals (body oils discolor them). In a ventilated entryway, many more can be safely used.

Denise says that reactions to her garland were split 90/10. "At intermission, people on the audience floor waved and blew kisses up to my box. Days later, I received notes from people I've never met, thanking me for the gesture. That minority 10 percent was nothing more than sour grapes."

"What about those people I read about whose eyes turned red," I asked.

"They weren't red; they were green with envy," she responded.

One in ten? She has a point.

Oh Sweet Pea,
My Sweet Pea

B ecause the English so obviously cherish the sweetly
scented annual, most people believe that the sweet pea
originated in Britain. In fact, it was discovered in the mid-
seventeenth century by a monk out on a ramble in Sicily.
The English didn't get their hands on it until early the following century. Even then, development was slow, mainly
because it's difficult to start sweet pea seed outdoors in the
cruel British climate.

In 1870, however, seeds fell into the hands of Henry
Eckford, a man who realized the sweet pea's full potential.
The Gloucestshire gardener was so convinced of its commercial value that he abandoned his career in order to work
full-time cross-fertilizing sweet peas in his Shropshire back-
yard. His single-mindedness paid off, for thirty years later
he had hybridized half of the 264 new sweet pea varieties
introduced in the Bicentenary Sweet Pea Exhibition.

By the beginning of the nineteenth century, the English
were insatiable in their pursuit of new sweet pea varieties.
Wavy petals appeared, flowers grew larger, and new colors
burst forth. As fragrance was thought to be far less important

than hue, varieties of sweet pea with no detectable bouquet abound today. But many others, thankfully, are magnificently aromatic.

Sweet peas are members of the *Leguminosae* family, and a genus of more than a hundred species. Only one, however, is perfumed—*Lathyrus odoratus*. This fragrant version comes in many hues, including red, salmon, pink, lavender, near blue, and white. After ordering catalogs from sweet pea specialists, ask only for those varieties called heavily perfumed or strongly scented. You'll seldom be able to smell those that are called lightly aromatic.

Sweet peas can be started directly in the earth when, as they say, "the ground can be worked"—meaning that you can stand to be outdoors to garden and that weather forecasters aren't predicting another frost.

Sunset magazine suggests a planting technique I like. It's also welcome news to those who don't like to do a lot of ground preparation, as it means digging a 6-inch-wide, 1-foot-deep trench in which all soil amendments are added. Get rid of one third of the soil you remove—unless it's not very good garden soil, in which case get rid of all of it and use a packaged all-purpose soil mix. One third of the refill mixture should be peat moss or sawdust. Be sure to add a good shot of balanced fertilizer such as 20-20-20 or Triple 15.

You can get a jump on the season by starting seeds indoors in biodegradable mesh starting pods. One more hint: Soak seeds overnight before planting them. To increase germination rate, nick each seed with a sharp knife, just enough to break the skin, before soaking it. A few drops of liquid fertilizer in the soaking water won't hurt either.

As if sweet peas weren't wonderful enough on their own, they better their mark by improving the soil they're planted in. They do what is known as "fixing" nitrogen in the soil—they deposit growth hormones that benefit later plantings.

To get the longest possible stems, you must follow a technique perfected in the early 1900s by an English gardener. He found that by identifying the main stem of a sweet pea early on and removing any wasted side growth, stems grow to 18 inches or longer and produce multiple flowers.

The only trick to producing lots of blooms should be welcome news—harvest the flowers regularly. If you don't, vines go to seed and stop blooming in order to concentrate instead on reproducing themselves. During midsummer, you should be picking blooms every other day, perhaps daily in a hot spell. The plants won't mind, and your diligence will keep them in bloom.

Lilium, the Fragrant

Except for roses, no flower is more strongly steeped in history than the lily. *Lilium candidum*, the cloyingly fragrant madonna lily, was thought to have sprung from the milk of Juno. When purity was the finest of virtues, white lilies were regarded as the epitome of grace, and old masters painted their regal forms while poets extolled their glories.

Not all lilies are fragrant; in fact, Gertrude Jekyll accused *L. pyrenaicum* of smelling like a mangy dog. The species and varieties that are actually pleasantly perfumed, however, cleverly make up for their scentless kin, and although many people believe that lilies rank just under tuberoses on a scale of perfume power, not everyone finds the scent of fragrant lilies agreeable. A seventeenth-century gardener who esteemed many flowers as cures for ailments said of *Lilium:* "Notwithstanding the sweet and delicious odour of the Lily of the garden, it becomes deleterious when freely inhaled in an apartment. Grave accidents and even death itself is reported to have resulted from individuals having remained exposed to the emanations of Lily flowers during the night." Many people still find the scent of lilies refreshing in an open garden overpowering in a closed room.

When you mention lilies to most people, they think of Easter and pots of *L. longiflorum* that have been forced under glass to bloom whenever the full moon and vernal equinox occur. *L. longiflorum* has little modesty where perfume is concerned, smelling irresistibly of jasmine, with maybe a touch of honey. Although some forms are native only to Okinawa, *L. longiflorum* is grown commercially all over the world. To make certain that no pollen will blemish their dazzling pure-white color, some growers remove each blossom's terra-cotta-to-crimson anthers before they have a chance to ripen, spill, and stain.

If you mention lilies to florists, they'll brag about their *L. speciosum*, the 'Rubrum' lily. Forms within this species may be pure white or seductive pink spotted with crimson purple. Whatever their color, most are powerfully fragrant. Since *L. speciosum* grows well under glass, the blooms are available for purchase throughout the year.

My personal favorites of the lily clan (because their perfume is the quintessence of lily) are commonly known as oriental lilies—modern hybrids of *L. auratum, L. speciosum, L. japonicum,* and *L. rubellum.* Unlike most lilies, which prefer sun or no more than high shade, oriental lilies appreciate shade—as much as a half day where summers are hot. They should also be planted deeper than most other lilies.

Lilies should be grown in neutral or slightly acidic soil (a pH between 5.5 and 6.5 is ideal). Good drainage is essential; otherwise, bulbs rot. If you buy your bulbs from specialists, instructions will accompany your order, telling you how deep to plant (bulbs that develop roots on stems that grow above the bulb's crown must be planted more deeply than others).

Keep beds of lilies well mulched. Where winters are hard, mulch softens the blow from sudden freezes. Where summers are hot, mulch keeps plants cool. Besides, *Lilium* species need nutrients if their bulbs are expected to multiply, and mulch, particularly leaf mold, provides plenty. Since lilies grow constantly, they should be kept well watered and always at root level, since sprinkling the foliage encourages the spread of disease spores.

Lilies are favorites for container planting, not just because they grow well in pots, but also because they don't naturalize easily. Where lilies grow contentedly, however, they multiply, but don't lift and divide them prematurely; wait instead until one year's bloom is noticeably skimpier than the last and stems are distinctly shorter. Then, separate bulbs after all foliage has turned yellow and congratulate yourself for growing lilies to perfection.

Want Butterflies?
Plant Buddleia

∞

In *The Scented Garden,* Rosemary Verey writes: "Shrubs of the genus *Buddleia,* being mostly vigorous and hardy, are too easy and accommodating to receive the attention they deserve." Those words are sweet music to the ears of overworked gardeners; self-reliant plants such as these give us extra time for those that need constant babying.

Buddleia was discovered in China in 1869 by a French missionary, Père Armand David. He lent his name to the species *Davidii,* but named the genus in honor of Rev. Adam Buddle, an early-eighteenth-century botanist. Today, there are more than a hundred species, though *Buddleia Davidii* is still the most popular, with numerous varieties available in colors from white to deep violet.

Buddleia shrubs are elegant and fast growing. If planted in sandy loam in full sun, a plant you buy in a 1-gallon container will easily grow to 8 feet in one season. Foliage is gray-green and willowlike, with leaves up to 9 inches long. Tiny flowers appear in crowded masses that form long conical sprays. All are sweetly aromatic, with honey being the prevalent scent. Lush, full blooms appear in early summer. There is often a second, though inferior, bloom in fall.

Buddleia is also known as the butterfly bush. You'll see why if you admit just a single plant to your garden—when buddleias first begin to release their honey musk in early summer, butterflies you never saw before will suddenly cruise your garden in packs. Monarchs and swallowtails will converge on the plants, adding striking color contrasts to a bush already in full bloom. Many people make a point of planting buddleias outside their windows so they can enjoy both their delicious scents, wafted indoors on soft summer breezes, and the sight of fat butterflies weighing down floriferous spikes.

Beware of gardeners who speak of pruning plants "to the ground." One cringes, hearing about how they hacked down their roses, magnolias, and wisteria—plants deserving more moderate treatment. *B. Davidii,* however, must be lopped off at the ankles each spring before new growth appears. Believe me, I know: When I planted my first buddleias, I pruned only lightly; the first year plants had delighted everyone with their prolific, irresistible blooms, and I wanted still more. A short way into the following season, I realized that I would pay for greed when bushes shot up to heights of more than 10 feet and half that wide. To cap it off, blooms were skimpy.

Another species, *B. alternifolia,* can be trained into a handsome, weeping willow–like tree. You must identify the plant's leading shoot early on (it will be the noticeably thicker one) and cut out all others until the trunk reaches 5 feet. The shoots that develop above this height will form dense heads that by midsummer will be covered in lavender-spiked flowers with an aroma like heliotrope. Prune *B. alternifolia* immediately after it blooms, keeping eyes ever on the watch for maintaining the desired weeping-tree shape.

Finally, there's *B. Fallowiana,* the most fragrant of all varieties. Its foliage is so closely covered with fine hairs that the plant takes on a silvery cast, providing a complementary background for the pale lavender–blue panicles of bloom.

Each spring, most buddleia liberally scatter their seed. These youngsters are welcome, of course, but be forewarned that they may not blossom the same color as their parent. For instance, I grow a white variety of *B. Davidii* that's my pride and joy. When I spotted its offspring, I was delighted, and gave plants away with promises of pristine white blooms. Alas, all seedlings reverted to buddleia's most prevalent color, lavender purple.

The butterflies, of course, didn't care.

The Extended Benefits of Culinary Wreaths

Ten years ago, I received an invitation to a holiday party I was dying to attend. A note in bold print at the bottom of the handsomely printed invitation, however, gave me pause: *Please bring a gift you made yourself.*

I've always been a dud in arts and crafts. Still, I had no intention of missing that party. I walked to the garden for inspiration.

Little was in bloom, of course, because it was early December and plants had endured a couple of frosts strong enough to crumple tender annuals such as nasturtium, basil, and nicotiana. Then, I noticed hedges of bay, myrtle, and rosemary, which looked terrific except for badly needed haircuts. I figured even a klutz could make a culinary wreath, and I gave it a shot. I've been making them ever since.

Culinary wreaths aren't merely a delight to the kitchen and the cooks who hold court there, they're agreeable anywhere a zesty herbal scent is welcome. Best of all, they're a snap to make. All you need is a supply of herbs, a form, thin florist's wire, and a pair of wire cutters.

No herb is prettier fresh or tastier dried than bay. Leaves harvested from healthy plantings of *Laurus nobilis,* the true culinary bay, remain dark green and lustrous for six weeks or longer. When foliage starts to dry, it's still fragrant and a delicious addition to a world of soups, stews, sauces, and marinades.

Next to bay, it's hard to beat rosemary for durability. Sprigs of rosemary are pungent with essential oils that remain sticky to the fingers long after being cut.

As far as I and the majority of cooks I know are concerned, you could call it quits once you have bay and rosemary. On the other hand, when you have ready supplies of marjoram, oregano, thyme, sage, or curry plant, bundles of their sprigs look good, too, especially if, in anticipation of frost, you've already dried them in little bunches.

Dark-green wreath forms in an assortment of sizes are readily available from crafts shops and retail floral suppliers. If you want to keep the project simple, buy flat forms; if you want to gild the lily, buy pinecone wreath forms, which have hollow cavities for harboring other fragrant plant materials, such as pelargonium or lemon verbena.

Fresh materials should be wired onto the form in batches with strands of 22- to 26-gauge florist's wire wrapped in a paddle. Holding the paddle of wire in the palm of one hand, use your other hand to hold culinary greens in place, looping wire toward the bottom of each bunch. The loose foliage of the next batch will help camouflage its predecessor's wire. Once wreath forms are thoroughly swathed in greens, it's time to add decorative elements—a bow, sprigs of fresh herbs, or clusters of garlic or peppers.

Because they're tailor-made for the job, the easiest way to attach decorative elements is to use florist's picks, which look like flat toothpicks with loose wire at one end. The wire serves to bind decorative materials to the wooden pick, which is then inserted into the wreath.

In retrospect, I'm mostly pleased with the single home-made accomplishment of my life. I need to shear hedges at year's end anyway, and it seems a shame to toss clippings onto the compost heap. Still, I realize that cooks to whom I offer these gifts will never let me off the hook. During summer, they tell me that last year's wreath is now on the back of a pantry door, but still redolent of aroma and flavor. By November, I hear word of a last leaf being put to superb gastronomical use. Sometimes I'm even invited to these feasts.

Brew a Batch of
Potpourri

I 've never understood why some gardeners devoted to fragrant plants imagine they must forego perfume throughout winter. What's wrong with potpourri until the fresh stuff's back around?

These suffering gardeners probably deprive themselves because they suspect their gardens aren't large enough to produce potpourri. Nonsense. The tiniest of yards, even sundeck container plants, yield plenty of material for drying (enough for gifts, too).

Not because they're my pets, but rather because their petals are so easy to work with, roses are irrevocably associated with potpourri. Other mainstays include lavender, a host of herbs, and the pungent leaves of certain trees, such as bay.

If you decide to blend potpourri from these regulars (or any plants that strike your fancy), first, harvest at the right moment—any time for roses, but herbs only during peaks of flavor. Certain herbs, such as dill and angelica, signal harvestime by forming heads of flower buds. Otherwise, taste for yourself; if your tongue sizzles, so will your nose.

Second, choose a spot for drying your bounty that's out of the sun, which bleaches colors and depletes essential oils. If you dry only small amounts, newspapers work well, especially laid over carpeting. When you run out of floor space (you can harbor lots under beds), don't even consider stacking fresh materials on top of those already drying because fresh petals mildew from lack of ventilation. Also, stay on the lookout for old window screens, which make perfect drying racks.

Plants such as lavender, rosemary, and thyme should be left on their stems, bundled together, then tied onto clothes-lines strung at the rear of dark closets. Whole flowers dry nicely, too, including heads of miniature roses, but they take longer to dehydrate than individual petals do.

Once you've accumulated enough dried materials for a recipe, declare your favorite spices and learn about fixatives and essential oils. Not only do fixatives actually have the inherent ability to absorb scented oils and suspend them in time, they also contribute a distinct scent of their own. Most fixatives are derived from resins and sold by names such as sandalwood, tonka beans (never grind them in your coffee mill), cedarwood, patchouli, storax, benzoin, and the ever-popular orrisroot.

Essential oils, distilled by nature or synthesized by man, determine each blend's final fragrance. For some fragrances, such as almond, coconut, eucalyptus, certain orange, and mint, you can buy true oils for little more than the cost of synthetics. Others, such as rose and gardenia oils, cost a fortune if they're not synthetic.

Recipes for dry potpourri usually specify one tablespoon each of fixatives and spices for each quart of dried material. Mix well all dried materials and apply essential oils. Once thoroughly blended, store the mixture in an airtight, opaque container and promise to mix it thoroughly once a week for at least six weeks and never loose heart over fragrance until the mixture is thoroughly aged.

If you want your potpourri to last as long as possible, keep it sealed and out of direct sunlight. Open the container only when you want to enjoy the smell of its contents.

Many people insist that their homemade potpourri remain visible and available for tossing by hand to punch up its aromas. If you keep your potpourri in open bowls or baskets, you can help revive lost scents by occasionally removing the blend to a large porcelain (never metal) bowl, adding a few drops of alcohol (vodka is best), and tossing it with a wooden spoon.

In time, of course, all scents are lost and colors will fade. Time for a new batch.

Ingredients for Bay-Rose Potpourri

3 quarts rose petals	1 ounce ground nutmeg
12 torn bay leaves	¼ ounce cinnamon, ground or whole
1½ cup lavender blossoms	¼ ounce ground cloves
1 cup orange blossoms	1 ounce neroli fragrance
2 ounces orrisroot	(or ½ ounce oil of neroli)

PART 6

Garden Jewels

Blooming Fools

The longer I garden, the more fond I become of plants that expect less than their fair share of attention. It's not laziness, it's simply that I grow mostly roses—notorious crybabies that demand more than their rightful due from floriculture.

Among easygoing companion plants, I have only the nicest things to say about two perennial garden workhorses whose merits are relatively unsung in the United States but adored in Europe. If you have bare spots in your garden but don't care to worry over what you plant there, you, too, should take a look at *Erysimum* 'Bowle's Mauve' and *Gaura Lindheimeri*. Both expect little in return.

The first time I spotted a plant of Bowle's Mauve, I was assured that it was a new variety of *Cheiranthus* (better known as wallflower). Once I found plants for sale, I was told that pathologists discovered specific technical differences in ovary and fruit requiring reclassification of *Cheiranthus* 'Bowle's Mauve' into another genus to which it is closely related—*Erysimum*.

Plants of *Erysimum* 'Bowle's Mauve' form bushy mounds from whorls of blue-green ironclad foliage. Flower stalks

rise from these rosette-shaped leaves and elongate into tall
spikes of bloom. Individual flowers mature from purple buds
into clear, light-violet, ½-inch blossoms with four petals
surrounding a greenish-yellow button eye. As flowers wither,
new buds form in their places and racemes elongate.

Apparently, no one ever told Bowle's Mauve when it
was time to stop blooming—because it doesn't. Plants purchased in 3-inch liners begin to flower after only a month
in the ground and remain in steady bloom even after hard
frosts. In time, of course, plants with tendencies toward
leggy woody growth must be sheared to shape and to
encourage new growth. Many gardeners shear Mr. Bowle
each midsummer (while there's plenty of bloom elsewhere)
to ensure a good fall crop.

Gaura Lindheimeri is native to Louisiana, where I grew
up. My mother never permitted any in her garden. "Why
should I encourage a weed in my yard when I can see all I
want of it in those ditches just down the road," she used to
say. I'm not certain what the attitude toward gaura is in
Louisiana these days, but in the rest of the country, it's quite
positive.

Gaura forms crowded stands of erect, slender stems with
hairy, gray-green, willowlike foliage. From these clumps,
wiry stems develop that bear elongating panicles of pink
buds that open into 1-inch white flowers resembling tiny
white butterflies. Because only a few blossoms open at a
time, blooming is extended over a long season.

Although gaura appreciates as much sun as gardeners can muster, it tolerates poor soil, drought, and general neglect. Blossoms drop off cleanly when spent, but seed-bearing spikes should be cut to the ground anyway, not only to improve overall appearance, but also to discourage enthusiastic self-sowing.

An axiom among garden designers is that short plants should be placed at the front of a flower border and tall plants at the rear. Such rules are well and good until boredom sets in, when gaura becomes a lifesaver. gaura is to a flower border what a scrim is to the theater—something that partially conceals a scene but doesn't hide what goes on behind. Plants growing beyond gaura can be seen clearly, but appear all the prettier because of the translucent haze.

I have a hedge of the famous Gallica rose 'Complicata' that borders a road leading to my garden. When 'Complicata' blooms, it wouldn't matter what was planted nearby—you wouldn't notice it. That thrilling event, however, takes only six weeks each year, after which matters are strictly foliar. My hedge looked bleak from July through October.

Although I knew they'd have to fend for their lives, growing so near a hell-bent-for-survival rose, I planted gauras among the shrubs. They take over when 'Complicata' stops showing off. Even though they're invading a nearby ditch, I think my mother would approve.

How Lily Regained the
Lotus Position

∽

When I left southwest Louisiana, I swore I never wanted
to see another water lily as long as I lived. I grew up
in bayou country, where water lilies clog waterways every
year and high school students are paid to haul them away in
gunnysacks that once held oysters.

For a few boyish years, each spring, I felt kindly toward
the lilies; their first blooms were perky and brightly colored
lavender blue, and the masses of leaves they floated above
seemed well contained. By midsummer, I remembered why
everyone cursed them so. Lavender blue turned murky
mauve and voracious foliage browned after it spread to
shore. I despised those lilies.

Years later, when I became so settled in the garden that
I decided to install a permanent fountain, someone suggested I use water lilies in its small pool. "Fat chance," I
thought to myself. I wanted lotus.

No flower is more steeped in history than the lotus. Not
even records of the early cultivation of the rose predate
those of *Nelumbo*. Egyptians chose the lotus to fashion head-
dresses for their sphinxes. In India and Tibet, the lotus was

considered so revered that Buddha himself is traditionally found sitting upon one of its blossoms, specifically *Nelumbo nucifera,* the sacred lotus. Pale-pink flowers shaped not unlike Hybrid Tea roses have a strong scent, also similar to that of roses. There is a Japanese variety, Alba Grandiflora, which blooms huge, pure-white, deliciously scented flowers; and a Chinese Pekinensis Rubra, whose rich red goblet-shaped blossoms are pungent with perfume.

I agonized for weeks over which varieties to try and finally settled on four. It will do me no good to describe the color or scent of their blossoms because I never got to scrutinize either. My lotus plants were a flop. No one, not even the catalog writer from where I ordered my fancy *Nelumbo,* told me that lotus thrive only in still water. I'm not sure whether it was the current in the pond or the trickles of water from the fountain that did my lotus in, but their pitiful pads never developed beyond the size of silver dollars, and flower buds never reached the water's surface. My pool stood empty.

Then, a friend who's nuts about water plants told me I had to get over this water lily aversion, that there was a great deal more to *Nymphaea* (water lily's proper name) than those vile bayou lilies.

What a world! Exotic water lilies are so different from the common ones of my youth that they barely seem related. First, exotic water lilies don't droop their roots in the water; they're planted in pots submerged more than a foot under the surface. Second, running water doesn't faze them. Finally, several of these lilies are wondrously colored and divinely scented, including: *Nymphaea albida,* the largest of all water lilies, with exotically fragrant pure-white blossoms that look as though they've been waxed; *N. capensis,* the African royal water lily, with rich blue, sharply fragrant star-shaped blooms; *N. odorata,* particularly 'Gigantea', whose blossoms look and smell like ice-white peonies; *N. caerulea,* the blue lotus of the Nile; and *N. tuberosa,* whose pure-white blossoms reach 6-inch widths and smell like ripe apples.

Purveyors of fine water lilies sell you everything you need in addition to the tubers themselves, including the pots. What you must always order is food designed specifically for water plants—tabs that are pressed into each pot at the beginning of blooming seasons and periodically throughout.

My pool still has a quick current and the water from the fountain still trickles, but I grow terrific water lilies. Even so, someday—when I have a still pond—I want to try lotus again.

Reflections on a Pond

When I decided to install a pond four years ago, the only plants I considered were water lovers—lotus, water lilies, certain irises, and maybe a cattail or two. Although I knew I wanted a couple of willow trees, I hadn't a clue what else to plant around the pond's perimeter. Fortunately, my friend Bob Galyean did.

"I know you think they're overdone and corny," he said, "but have you ever spent time near a pond encircled with ornamental grasses? Some of them nod toward water more gracefully than any plant I know and others are stiffly upright—perfect as a background.

"Not entirely grasses," he continued. "That would be boring. You've already admitted to wanting willows, but a few forsythias would be nice, too," reminding me that forsythias are the quintessential flowering pond plant because they blossom so early and nod their branches smack down to water surfaces, maximizing their reflection.

The handwriting was on the wall; Bob had a much clearer image of what this pond should look like than I did. Although I wasn't swept away with the prospect of grasses, ornamental or not, I took his advice. Thank goodness I did.

I got my willow trees, two of them. First, *Salix baby-lonica,* the classic weeping willow that can reach 50 feet with even greater spread. The second willow, and my personal favorite, is *Salix umbraculifera,* commonly known as the globe willow. Capable of reaching 35 feet with equal spread, the globe willow matures into a round, umbrella-shaped head with drooping branchlets.

Next came the forsythias, three plants of *Forsythia* x *intermedia* strategically placed for maximum light and reflec-tion. Then, just to assure that the pond area related to the rest of the garden, Bob scattered plants of Portugal laurel, viburnum, and buddleia—all signature plants of the garden at large—around the pond.

With the permanent plants in place, it was time to con-sider the grasses. I imagined a selection of six or so; Bob had forty-eight in mind. I haven't grown to love them all, but several have won my heart, including most of the forms of *Miscanthus,* which undergo dramatic color changes as winter approaches. *Miscanthus sinensis* 'Purpurascens', for instance, changes from reddish green to flaming orange, then finally to attractive shades of reddish brown.

I'm partial to the festuca grasses, too. Varieties such as *Festuca amethystina,* for instance (which borders almost one quarter of the pond's perimeter), sports elegant spiky foliage that leans over just enough to graze water surfaces. *Cortaderia Selloana* 'Evita' is even more graceful and bears festive golden seed heads each fall that darken to amber as they mature. My very favorite is *Miscanthus sinensis* 'Yaku-Jima', which, at the slightest breeze, thrusts 4 inches of its pointed leaves under water.

To obtain height for background plantings, you needn't consider the ubiquitous pampas grasses, although several are worth a second look. *Cortaderia Selloana* 'Pumila', for instance, is a 4- to 6-foot version of the 20-foot giant pampas grass. Another smashing staunchly erect ornamental grass is *Arundo Donax* 'Versicolor Superba', whose dense swordlike leaves are dramatically striped green and yellow.

My fondness for ornamental grasses is due to far more than their variety of color, height, and seed-bearing abilities—their intolerance of disease and fuss-free growth habits are a joyous addition to the garden. True, most need to be sheared to the ground late each winter, but spring's sprightly growth is right behind.

Of all seasons, however, I most love ornamental grasses in autumn, when my pond is encircled with varieties 4 feet taller than I am. When I stand on the small bridge over the center of that pond, I feel like I'm in a handsomely decorated private room.

Patiently Waiting
Just for Yew

∽

W hen I was choosing among plants to form a hedge along one side of my garden, I turned to a fine gardening consultant for advice.

"Tell me, do you ever want to photograph plants in front of the hedge?" he asked (knowing full well that I did), then said I should consider nothing other than yew.

"But yews are so poky," I protested. "I want pictures *during* my lifetime."

My horticultural guru went on to explain that, yes, yew are exceptionally slow growing but that no other evergreen hedging plant responded better to manicuring or remained more evenly colored lush green. "Besides," he said, "yews like to be pruned during your birthday month of August. All in all, I think yew are definitely you."

The Leo aspect was flattering, but just as appealing was growing a plant requiring attention on a memorable date. I've always liked the fact that daffodils should be planted the day after Thanksgiving and that roses appreciate being pruned by Valentine's Day. I resolved to have patience while my yews took their own sweet time forming a proper hedge. The wait was worthwhile.

Depending on how they're pruned, yews (*Taxus* is their Latin name) are evergreen trees or shrubs that respond uncommonly well to shearing. Although yews are technically conifers, female plants bear tiny poisonous fruit (I've never met a person or known an animal who could stand more than a taste) instead of cones.

The classic yew, *Taxus baccata,* commonly known as English yew, is the true species, but garden varieties are far more common, particularly *Taxus baccata* 'Stricta' (Irish yew), which has larger leaves than English yew.

Once established, yews are notably drought tolerant. While maturing, however, yews appreciate regular waterings. Although not fussy over soil (unless it's extremely acidic or alkaline), yews insist on good drainage.

After tending plants for a while, gardeners come to appreciate those as impervious to diseases and insects as yew plants. Other than root rot (caused by soggy ground), yews contract no diseases I know of, and the only insects bold enough to attack the plants are scale and spider mites. When spider mites are detected (look for tiny spider webs at the base of plants anytime summer temperatures soar), you can kill two birds with one stone by giving plants a thorough soak from top to bottom with a garden hose. Spider mites can't stand water, but thickets of yew love a long cold shower during hot weather.

For those too impatient to wait for yews to mature, you should know that established plants (even trees) transplant well. Know also, however, that your impatience will cost you a pretty penny. No nursery that has pampered the plants for the twenty or so years it takes them to form a perfect sentinel is going to sell them for a song.

The yews I planted eight years ago were only 1 foot tall when I nestled their tiny bushes into well-prepared, fast-draining soil just in front of my neighbor's unsightly 3½-foot barbed-wire fence. In three years, they reached 3 feet. Now, at a lofty 5 feet, they entirely camouflage that fence.

Figuring that their fragile new growth needed pampering, not discipline, I never touched those yews with pruning shears during their first two years in my ground. After the third year, however, it was clear that sheering was in order, and I've since clipped them annually within a week of my birthday.

That advice regarding photography was right on, by the way. I still don't photograph any nearby flowers on plants taller than 5 feet, but when blossoms occur on shorter branches, it's hard to imagine improving on their background—in the garden or on film.

Haws, Hips, Berries, and Fruits

∞

A recent visitor to my garden asked why I grow hawthorn trees when I'm an avowed devotee of perfumed plants. "*Crataegus* are in the aminoid family of fragrance," she reminded me, "and most people think they actually stink, or at least smell fishy."

I reminded my guest that varieties such as the elegant pure-white *Crataegus Phaenopyrum* emit a balsamic fragrance when flowers are fresh. "Besides," I added, "I don't grow hawthorns just for their blossoms; their haws are smashing."

Hawthorns are but one of a host of plants whose ornamental fruits are treasured almost as much as its blossoms. Roses, of course, head the list. The fruits of rosebushes, called hips, are actually seedpods that mature after blossoms fade. Although they can be harvested for seeds, hips are more treasured as a potent source for vitamin C and for decorative effects once blossoms are but memories of last summer.

The hips of most rosebushes are red or orange, but some, such as those of *Rosa Hugonis* and *R. pimpinellifolia,* are black.

Size varies, too. Hips on Rambling roses are usually small, but those on certain shrub varieties such as *R. rugosa*

'Scabrosa' may reach the size of crab apples. If elegant shapes appeal to you, by all means have a look at the hips on R. *Moyesii* (and its several forms) and R. *macrophylla*— they're shaped like flagons.

Many gardeners believe that modern roses don't form hips, but several of today's hybrids do. 'Bonica', for instance, the first Landscape rose to win the coveted All-America Rose Selection award (1987), produces scads of clear-orange plump hips as long as you leave the last roses of summer on the bush. Only when blossoms are left to wither on their stems do rosebushes think it's proper to set seed. If you want hips, don't deadhead each season's last crop of blossoms.

Holly, or *Ilex,* is the most-familiar berry-producing garden plant, but if you grow it for its fruits instead of for its shiny green spiny foliage or insignificant (though sometimes fragrant) flowers, be certain that you grow the right variety. For instance, *Ilex cornuta* (Chinese holly) is famed for its exceptionally large, long-lasting, dazzling red berries, but only certain varieties, such as *I. cornuta* 'Dazzler', deserve that reputation. Others, such as *I. cornuta* 'Carissa', produce no berries at all.

Flowering crab apples, properly known as *Malus,* are reliable fruiters. Some varieties, such as M. 'Hopa' and M. 'Red Silver', serve double duty because their fruits are not only ornamental, they make delicious tart jelly. Others, such as M. 'Red Jade', aren't tasty but put on quite a show when they mass themselves on weeping branches.

Certain fuchsias are actually praised more for their fruit than for their flowers. The fine species *Fuchsia boliviana,* for instance, blossoms with clusters of pretty tubular flowers that pale in comparison to the shiny aubergine fruit that follows.

I grow a rectangular hedge of *Viburnum Tinus* 'Spring Bouquet' that I planted because of its notorious growth habits—dense foliage smack down to the ground, a natural for meticulous clipping. A nurseryman told me that the blossoms were richly scented, which proved to be an exaggeration (I have to hyperventilate before I can ever sniff its perfume). The berries of this viburnum variety, however, are another matter. Although most gardening books say that the fruits are metallic blue (meaning that they're shaded gray and black), those that form out of direct sunlight are often pure lapis blue.

If you know a flower arranger you want to stay on the good side of, by all means try some of these fruit-producing plants. They'll praise you for hawthorn haws, bless you for viburnum berries, and act downright reverant over the hips of 'Bonica'.

Personalizing Pumpkins

B ack when I was first getting my garden off the ground, I kept a compost pile along one perimeter. One year, when I had more than enough for mulching beds of roses and perennials, I was left with a heap of compost too rich to ignore.

"I'll just camouflage the mound with quick-growing vines," I said to myself, "and use that compost next season, when it will be all the richer for decomposing another year." Since there was plenty of room for vines to sprawl, I sowed vegetables that I knew would appreciate the space— zucchini, assorted squashes, and pumpkins, all of which so loved the fertile loam that they produced bumper crops.

The following season, when I needed the compost on hand, I realized that my garden had no more space for viny gourds. "Get over it," I said to myself. "Gourds take up too much room—buy them at the market." Although I took my advice to heart, no squash I bought that year tasted as good as those from the garden the year before, neither were they as appealingly formed. I missed pumpkins most of all.

While completing my order for vegetable seeds last year, I came across the fetchingly named Cinderella pumpkin.

Once I decided that I had to grow it, no matter how much space it required, I walked into the garden to find a blank spot and discovered one in a bed of asparagus.

The key to growing good gourds is not finding room for planting their seeds, but rather providing space for their vines to mature. The asparagus bed was ideal; not only was it raised, thereby providing excellent drainage, it was located adjacent to paths between rows of annuals and perennials growing in a cutting garden. "Plenty of room to spread along the sides," I declared one fine day in May.

My scheme worked as long as I kept pace with the rambunctious Cinderella. By the end of the growing season, it trailed longer than 30 feet. When errant vines traipsed across paths (forcing one to tiptoe rather than stroll), I used bricks or weighty rocks to secure them back in place. In a few days, they stayed put.

Since I was after quality rather than quantity, once the pumpkins matured to the size of oranges, I removed all but three or four per vine, thereby concentrating all energy into my chosen few. By October, they were outrageous; several weighed more than 50 pounds each.

My unconventional training method resulted in another advantage: Because the paths were covered in loose gravel that drained well, the pumpkins stayed dry and never developed those unsightly dark blotches that form when gourds are expected to ripen on damp soil.

A friend taught me another pumpkin trick. "While

maturing pumpkins still have soft buttery skins, you can scratch on designs that will callus permanently as the pumpkins age," she assured me. "Grab a Phillips screwdriver and get creative."

The trick to pumpkin scratching is beginning with the right varieties, specifically those with soft skins such as Big Max (which can grow to over 100 pounds) or Little Boo (which rarely grows heavier than 8 pounds but is beautifully colored ivory to pale yellow).

If you want to test your design before making it irreversible, use a ballpoint pen to lightly sketch what you intend to scratch in. Also, decide if your midsummer message will still please you in October. For reasons best known to me one summer, I thought "Trick or Treat" would be clever in fall, also "Boo." By Halloween, they looked silly. This year, I'm going to try my hand at drawing spiderwebs.

Callused from scratching or not, I won't be without homegrown pumpkins again.

Camellia—The Queen of Winter Flowers

When people tell me that they're sick to death of the ubiquitous Christmas poinsettia and that they yearn for fresh-cut garden flowers to bring indoors, I always suggest adding camellias to their garden. Considering that camellia hybridizing is yet in its infancy and there are already 3,000 separately named varieties, few flowers match camellias for range of color or form, and nothing equals them for bountiful winter bloom, including varieties that strut their stuff just in time for the holidays.

Although there are many from which to choose, gardeners usually settle on varieties of only one species—*Camellia japonica,* the quintessential camellia. When planting a named variety of *C. japonica,* plan on it growing into a 6- to 12-foot shrub. Many plants are taller, of course (to more than 40 feet), but they're also a hundred years old.

Catalogs of camellias usually list varieties by season, noting whether they are early, midseason, or late bloomers. In California, early means October through January, midseason is January to March, and late is March to May.

Like roses, camellias come in every color but blue (that may change soon, say ambitious hybridizers). Flower form is widely varied, too—single, semidouble, and fully double. Some varieties have blossoms that resemble peonies, anemones, or roses; others have petals with fringed edges and some that resemble floppy rabbit ears.

Camellias require specific culture—organically rich, well-drained soil in shady areas. Older plants are able to grow in full sun, but that's because they have developed a thick canopy of foliage to shelter their roots from parching sun. Most new plants require time to provide shade on their own; in the meanwhile, grow them under tall trees, lath, or on the north side of buildings. Never plant the trunk base of a camellia plant below ground level, and don't allow soil to wash over it later; use a friable carpet of mulch instead.

Camellias are heavy feeders and their diet is specific—acidic. Plants should be fed with commercially formulated acid fertilizer, generally after blooming. Never apply more fertilizer than the label calls for. If you're the sort of gardener who likes to fertilize and water by hand often (it *is* enjoyable, but still work), cut dosages in half and feed twice as often as the manufacturer says you should.

When camellia plants are in trouble, they signal their pain through their foliage. If the centers of leaves are yellowed or scorched, they're getting too much sun. If leaves burn at their edges or drop excessively, they're overfertilized. If leaves turn yellow but retain green veins, they're chlorotic, and drainage must be improved or plants fed with iron chelate.

Although they would just as soon be cut back immediately after flowering, camellias aren't fussy about pruning; summer and fall are okay, too. Whenever you prune, use common sense. Remove all dead wood as well as weak and spindly growth. As plants mature, thin out wood that interferes with the blossoms of adjacent stems.

Prune for the look you want. If plants are squat, shorten their lower branches to encourage upright growth; if plants are lanky, cut back top growth.

As shrubs mature, you'll have so many blossoms that you can afford to harvest blossoms with long stems. Keep in mind, of course, that such greedy behavior sacrifices the flower buds lower on the stem (they will open if left on the plant). If you can't afford the luxury of long stems, cut blossoms with short stems as they mature and float them in bowls of water. Personally, I'll take three sprays of camellias floating in a bowl rather than a potted poinsettia any day.

PART 7

'Tis the Season

Put Spring on Order

Although I fancied my garden's display of King Alfred daffodils last March, I was overcome with envy when I glanced next door. Instead of monotonous sheets of yellow daffodils, my neighbor's garden was resplendent with splashes of caressible ivory-white Mount Hood, cuddly pink Passionale, juicy apricot Petit Four, and the dazzling orange miniature Jetfire. For the umpteenth year in a row, I had dillydallied with my order for spring bulbs until forced to plant substitutes instead of first choices. I vowed to change my ways and am pleased to report that I just received confirmation that my coveted requests for next year's spring bulbs will soon be shipped.

After deciding the companies from which I'm going to order bulbs, I make three copies of each order form. I fill out the first duplicate in total disregard for cost, reveling instead in the collection I've imaginatively assembled. Then, I total the cost of my dream order. When I recover from the shock of the price for living out my fantasy, I pare down the list of the second draft, although it, too, is consistently beyond my budget. By the time I hone my third order, I start getting real. Do I *really* need the entire collection of new peony tulips, or won't that deep-rose May Wonder and the stunning black-red Uncle Tom do the job? Once I reach the height of practicality, just before filling out the supplier's original order form, I give preference to those bulbs that will continue to satisfy me year after year.

I wish I could tell you that recently introduced tulips and hyacinths number among naturalizers, but they don't. These Dutch beauties were hybridized to withstand cruel winters, and as a result they persist over time only in such climates. Daffodils, on the other hand, make terrific investments, multiplying their bulbs annually. Five years ago, when someone who seemed well informed told me that daffodils repel gophers, I planted 2,000 bulbs. Last year, when I could no longer ignore that they were overcrowded (signified by one year's bloom being noticeably skimpier than the last), I bit the bullet and divided my daffodil collection. Although I lost track of the number of bulbs I lifted, then replanted, I'm certain that my original planting had quadrupled. To my great disappointment, by the way, I learned that daffodils don't deter gophers one bit. Although daffodil bulbs are poisonous to gophers, the voracious monsters simply nose them out of the way toward something that isn't.

Another misinformed horticulturist told me that crocuses multiply like rabbits. Not for me, although I've been assured that crocuses actually do naturalize in climates colder than mine. The good news for us gardeners in temperate climates is that crocuses are so cheap that it's not unbearable to consider buying them anew each year. Keep in mind, however, that you should plant masses of crocuses rather than just a few. Crocuses look wonderful growing in lawns just under the spread of a large, deciduous tree, but only if they take up at least half the space.

Speaking of good investments, don't overlook Muscari, better known as grape hyacinth. Not only are they deliciously scented of honey-musk, Muscari plants are garden gadabouts—adaptable wherever they grow, carefree multipliers, and oblivious to the soil in which they're planted. Although most Muscari plants are short and fat and bloom in shades of lavender or blue, some are tall, skinny, and pure white.

I plant bulbs as soon as I can get to them after they arrive, except for the big trio—daffodils, tulips, and hyacinths, which I plant the day after Thanksgiving. Besides having the day off, planting bulbs is a welcome chore for working off that extra slab of turkey that someone forced me to eat. As for the reputed advantage of refrigerating bulbs in the meantime, that's an old wives' tale; just store them in a cool, dry, dark closet.

There's nothing sacred about the last week in November, of course. Plant whenever it's convenient or when balmy weather beckons you outdoors. Whatever else you do to avoid another ho-hum spring, however, order bulbs *now*. Otherwise, it's back to King Alfreds.

Summer Hors d'Oeuvres

Summer gardens remind me of cocktail parties with open bars. Like butterflies drunk from squatting on fat blooms of honey-scented buddleia, I'm woozy over cloying perfumes from heady honeysuckle. Before summer's bonanza fades, Mexican evening primroses and mullein climb out of their beds and into paths; mint entirely takes over a neighbor's rightful home; seedlings of lavender pop up in unlikely places; and Rugosa roses send up shoots yards away from their mother plants.

Gardeners who've attended such giddy gatherings know a hangover is just around the corner if they don't take action for easing out of summer. The job is twofold—to extend the life of the party and to plan for autumn's fiesta.

If you hold any hopes for keeping your summer garden party going, you have no choice but to serve food. I've never understood why some gardeners become complacent over fertilizer by midsummer. Where's fall's bounty to come from? That meal last spring is but a dim memory to a hungry rose. Any plant that flowers as often as roses do must have a steady diet of properly formulated fertilizer.

If the sizes of your midsummer rosebushes please you, but you yearn for larger, more vividly colored blossoms, let up on nitrogen (the first number in every fertilizer's trio of essential ingredients) and concentrate instead on phosphorus and potassium. Roses fed a midsummer meal of a fertilizer such as 6-20-20 show deep appreciation for the next six weeks (after which they should be fed again, this time with less nitrogen or none at all).

Annuals with an extended season of bloom need more help than fertilizers alone; they must be sheared back, too. Garden favorites such as delphinium, penstemon, gaura, pansy, lobelia, and allysum, for instance, have been in the ground a long time by midsummer and their plants look haggard. Hack them back and give them a good dose of all-purpose fertilizer like 20-20-20. Any plant ratty beyond redemption should be yanked and replaced with quick-action favorites like calendula, poppy, salvia, snapdragon, and stock.

It's always comforting to spot plants of chrysanthemum, aster, and sedum thriving in July because their inevitable blossoms ensure a colorful autumn. If you didn't get your plants in the ground during spring (when you should have), it's not too late; you'll simply pay for your oversight. By midsummer, most nursery plants have been removed from their spring sleeves or trays and repotted into 1-gallon containers. Your nursery, of course, deserves compensation for this care it gave in your stead. On the other hand, many nurseries stage terrific sales in late summer because they must reduce inventory in order to lower water bills.

Don't overlook the vegetable garden if you're worried about fall color. The bulk of ornamental vegetables are fall crops, and selections such as red Swiss chard and blue-leaved leeks are handsome companions for autumn's floral splendor.

I'm embarrassed to admit that I don't always take to heart the advice I so willingly offer (I do, however, follow all suggestions where proper rose culture is concerned). Still, I'm often that person behind you in line at the garden-center counter who also forgot to plant in spring with an eye toward fall. And many winters I'm left with vegetable seed I intended to sow before it was too late to consider anything but costly seedlings.

In any case, I figure that we gardeners are the ones throwing the party and we have a right to enjoy it. If you really don't mind zealous blooming fools crowding paths or tumbling to the ground from their mighty floriferous weight, then go for it—indulge yourself in decadence.

Another gin and tonic, please.

Autumn Joy

∞

W hen the calendar signals the approach of the autumn equinox, most gardeners pack up their trowels and call it a year. That's a pity, for autumn is a thoroughly satisfactory season among those horticulturists who recognize that there's more to fall than chrysanthemums, sedums, apples, and pumpkins.

Autumn is a fine time to be in the garden for the weather alone. The sublime bite to the morning air makes wearing a flannel shirt infinitely more pleasant than donning a visor to ward off July's harsh rays. Besides, there are inevitable chores to rid gardens of the spoils of summer's floral orgies, and autumn's snug warmth makes such jobs inviting.

Remember, too, that autumn is the very best season for transplanting herbaceous plants—daylilies, hostas, and a host of flowering perennials. Fall transplants have a head start on those hurried into the ground during spring, because their roots have a chance to settle and lay claim to their allotted home.

No season offers a broader tapestry of colors than autumn. Besides maples, elms, and liquid ambers whose foliage look like bonfires, complementary floral colors abound. First, garden standbys persist long past typically allocated bloom cycles—coreposis, erysimum, gaura, lavatera (tree mallow), and rudbeckia. The colors of some perennials actually improve noticeably over their summer selves, like gaillardia, whose hot hues become less startling than they were during August. Several salvias undergo an entire color transformation. You may wonder all summer, for instance, how Indigo Spires came by its name, but when autumn's sun wanes and evenings cool, these heady sage blossoms turn from ordinary blue to true indigo.

Annuals also deserve a rightful place in autumn's land-scape, and those gardeners who plant from seed (rather than depending entirely upon nursery selections) have a field day with choices, like cosmos, four o'clock, nigella (love-in-a-mist), and candytuft. Even California poppies, usually asso-ciated only with early summer, flower beautifully in fall if their seeds are sown during summer. Although they're few in number, some annuals bloom only in autumn, most notably vining moonflower and tithonia (more commonly known as Mexican daisies), whose velvety, reddish-orange, 3-inch blossoms make sensational cut flowers.

When one mentions bulbs to most gardeners, they think of spring bulbs that must be planted in fall. In fact, the botanical bulb world—corms, rhizomes, tubers, and bulbs themselves—stakes a mighty claim on bloom in the autumn garden. Besides the ubiquitous (and too often tacky) cannas, there are alliums (particularly the garlic chive), crocuses (most notably *Crocus sativus,* whose stigmas, when roasted, yield saffron), cyclamens, and dahlias.

It is, perhaps, the woody plants of autumn that serve fall gardens most dutifully—oak leaf hydrangea, pyracantha, cotoneaster, holly, viburnum, *Nandina domestica* (heavenly bamboo, which is technically neither angelic nor a true bamboo), elaeagnus, cotinus (smoke bush), and franklinia.

Finally, my pets—roses. At no season during the blooming year are roses more spectacular than in autumn. Assuming they've been given a decent meal of fertilizers in August, Indian summer roses have longer stems than any preceding them on the same bush, and their colors intensify as their blossoms enlarge.

On an evening in late October last year, I cased out my roses to decide whether to harvest blossoms that night or the next morning. I decided to wait, mostly because I figured nothing would be lost and the already oversized blooms would only improve. As it happened, there was a full harvest moon that night that was bright enough to read by. The roses cut the next morning were a sight to behold. Not only were they long stemmed, huge, and richly colored, they had extended vase life written all over them.

Autumn renders miracles like these from the equinox until long after Mother Nature pelts winter on our garden's parade. It would be a shame to miss it, indoors.

Winter Wonderland

E ach year, on the day I'm compelled to stop cutting
flowers because they're either waterlogged or frozen,
I call my travel agent to book a trip somewhere warm.
Although such indulgence appears selfish, for gardeners fac-
ing winter it's really not. Horticulturists need climactic
changes to remind us to be thankful that somewhere there
are gardens when ours go dormant. For a refresher course
in the other world, I go to Hawaii.

There's no denying that the floral extravaganza of the
Hawaiian Islands is a shoot-out—blazing croton, bougainvillea, poinciana trees, vining passionflowers, and orchids.
But, would you hand over your clematis for bougainvillea
or swap buddleia for croton? I certainly wouldn't.

Winter is vital to a gardener's favorite plants—wisteria,
viburnum, daphne, lilac, numerous bulbs, magnolia,
peonies, and roses. Where winter temperatures never drop
low enough to force these chill lovers into dormancy, many
literally bloom themselves to death.

People who understand their gardens inside out aren't
bothered by the fact that spring perennials stand nakedly leafless in winter. Quite the contrary, we bless the 20/20 vision

dormancy affords us for spotting those wisteria arms that can be lopped off to lighten the pergola's load or the precise stubborn rose cane, which, each July, snags us on the way to the tuberoses.

A treasured winter blessing is time for lounge chair gardening, when meaty catalogs become a gardener's salvation. On a blustery winter day when no person in his right mind would venture into the garden, guilt gets hustled out the door as we sit comfortably, poring over catalogs and reveling in the opportunity to commit to memory this year's needs in, say, the vegetable garden.

"If peas, beans, or any nitrogen-fixing legumes were planted there last year, then it's okay to move the tomatoes back to that bed," we assure ourselves, then ask, "Is it cucumber or zucchini that enhances the flavor of lettuce?" (Cucumber; plant the zucchini where the tomatoes were.)

There will, of course, be days when decent weather beckons you outdoors to admire those plants who strut their stuff only in winter—witch hazel, for instance. Witch hazel is something of an acquired smell. When you first see its flowers, you'll probably think that they're some sort of disfigured foliage and doubt whether they harbor any fragrance. If you bother to lean over to sniff them, your nose will change your mind, for the scent of witch hazel is incenselike, almost addictive.

Hellebores also reach their glory in winter and none more cheerfully than *Helleborus niger,* the Christmas rose (which may actually bloom on Christmas Day in some winter climates). The Christmas rose bears only a vague likeness to real heritage garden roses, but it's fetching.

Winter ushers in a host of other garden favorites—trees and shrubs like acacia, camellia, and forsythia; perennials like cymbidium and primula; bulbs like crocus and cyclamen; and even flowering annuals like certain calendula, linaria, and viola.

Remember also to keep in mind those flowers well past their season. If you haven't pruned, you may have surprises in store. Last Christmas, I went out into the garden with dim hopes of finding roses. Temperatures had dipped into the teens several nights during the previous week and it had rained besides. Most bushes had given up the ghost right after Thanksgiving. Then I thought to look near the south end of a shed where I had planted several bushes of 'Sally Holmes'—a little-known rose that deserves fame for non-stop production of sweetly scented, beige-white flowers formed in trusses, like rhododendron. Because of the luxurious reflected heat afforded by a southern exposure, these plants pretend they're in season even when they're not.

Since I was about to prune anyway, I ruthlessly cut 3-foot stems. It's true that petals were frostbitten and I had to shake blossoms upside down after harvesting since they were brimming with water, but once I put them in a large container, people looked at the Christmas tree only after they rolled their eyes over Sally.

A Gardener's
New Year's Resolutions

∞

S ince I'm from the bayou country of Louisiana, I'm among that hoard of southerners notorious for making New Year's resolutions (in Cajun country, resolutions play as big a part in the holidays as Santa Claus). Discouraged by poor performance in recent years, however, I've quit making lifestyle resolutions such as promising never to have a cocktail before 6 P.M. or eat french fries more than once a week. My garden, on the other hand, has benefited from my good intentions, although not always for the entire following year, of course.

This year, among my resolutions is the vow to keep every promise I make to the garden. Here they are:

Since they're my pets, roses will profit most. First, and because this particular promise must be kept soon, I resolve to do a thorough job of dormant spraying. Reason for spraying dormant rosebushes to rid them of leftover disease and insect spores has grown in recent years, thanks to a nationwide infestation of an offbeat rose disease called downy mildew (the name is thoroughly misleading because the disease itself has nothing to do with either down or mildew, but rather with purple blotches that appear on all plant parts, including hard wood). Downy mildew can be lethal; if it attacks young plants, it usually kills them. The only way to keep downy mildew out of your rose garden is to bar its entry with the use of zinc- or copper-based hydroxide sprays. I vow to spray every rosebush I have twice; once immediately after foliage is stripped off in preparation for pruning, and again right after bushes are pruned.

And I promise my roses never to stroll among them (except with guests, of course) without a pair of sharp shears. I have no idea how many times I've walked past a bush and spotted something that needed to come out right then. I'd make a mental note of where it was (intending to go back later), but would rarely spot that precise problem again.

To the garden at large, I promise to prune in a timely fashion. For reasons I can only attribute to laziness, my mock orange (*Philadelphus*) has become rangy because its plants weren't cut back right after they bloomed, when they should have been. Pruning seems wrong in summer, but many flowering shrubs such as quince and *Viburnum Opulus* should be sheared into shape as soon as they finish blossoming. Other garden standbys need summer pruning, too, such as yew (in August).

I'm also going to be timely with weeding. The preferred time for ridding gardens of oxalis and wild onions is the instant you see them growing. Fortunately, that moment occurs when noxious weeds are easy to yank because the ground they're choking is moist from spring rains.

I promise to stop living without bulbs I'm dying to grow. For instance, I've requested *Amaryllis Belladonna,* commonly known as naked-ladies, for the past two years, but they still don't flourish in my garden because I've waited too long to place my order. This year, I intend to act as soon as I see a naked-lady in bloom (late summer, when these bulbs should be ordered).

Finally, I'm going to be diligent about staggering vegetable crops, particularly butter lettuce and arugula. I'm crazy about arugula and it's so easy to grow that I have no good excuse for not having it to enjoy year-round, especially now that I have a greenhouse.

Those who know me well would probably attest that I'll keep these promises to roses, but scoff at my other timely pruning vows. But, I dare you to catch me without arugula.

Index